CHILDREN, TEACHERS, AND MATHEMATICS

Children, Teachers, and Mathematics

DAVID A. THOMAS
Montana State University

Allyn and Bacon
Boston   London   Toronto   Sydney   Tokyo   Singapore

Copyright © 1991 by Allyn and Bacon
A Division of Simon & Schuster, Inc.
160 Gould Street
Needham Heights, Massachusetts 02194

Library of Congress Cataloging-in-Publication Data

Thomas, David A. (David Allen), 1946–
    Children, teachers, and mathematics / David A. Thomas.
        p. cm.
    Includes bibliographical references.
    ISBN 0-205-12681-2
    1. Mathematics—Study and teaching (Elementary)—United States.
    I. Title.
    QA135.5.T493   1991
    372.7'0973—dc20   90-37820
                                                                              CIP

Printed in the United States of America

10 9 8 7 6 5 4 3 2 1   94 93 92 91 90

Contents

Preface

It happened during my sophomore year at college. Along with a hundred other students, I was enduring a physics lecture by one of the driest professors on campus. To all appearances, the students in the lecture hall were semiconscious.

The lecture started with a question: How much work is done in moving an electron "upstream" against an electric field? For the next fifteen minutes, the learned professor filled the chalkboard with equations and mathematical diagrams. The class followed his calculations sluggishly, counting the minutes until lunch.

As the professor neared the end of his mathematical meanderings, I suddenly sensed the ultimate destination of the presentation. My mind reeled. Without warning, I was being initiated into one of the mysteries of the universe. I started to tingle as, step by step, I reviewed the equations and diagrams and verified that I understood it all.

There it was. The *big* one: $E = mc^2$. Every student in the lecture hall sat bolt upright. The old professor had our attention.

Something happened to me that day. The revelation that great wonders were within my grasp transformed me. I stopped dreaming little dreams and, at least in spirit, became a scientist. Now, more than twenty years later, the power that inspired my classmates still awes me. It is the power of mathematics to describe and explain the mysteries of the universe, and it is the wonder of my own understanding. This, indeed, is something to be shared!

Children enter school interested in mathematics. To small children accustomed to counting and comparing quantities, mathematics is both real and practical. They know that mathematics can be used to determine whether a particular way of dividing treats awards each child the same number of candies, cookies, or the like. They also know that mathematics can be used to measure growth, which has its own rewards. Because they appreciate this kind of knowledge, many children enter school feeling that mathematics is both relevant and reasonable.

Unfortunately, the natural interest of preschool children in mathematics is not always extended and supported in school. All too often, a primary-grades mathematics curriculum focuses on abstract paper-and-pencil computation rather than concept development and problem solving. Such curricula train children to manipulate abstract symbols in complex ways (addition, subtraction, multiplication, and long-division exercises) in order to obtain "answers" to questions that are posed without reference to the real world. This approach separates all meaning from the act of finding sums, differences, products, and quotients; it treats arithmetic operations as abstractions to be mastered by rote memorization.

Children fed a steady diet of drill and practice may well become proficient at basic computation. What parents and teachers often fail to recognize is that this proficiency often comes at a high price: Many children subjected to such a curriculum will come to dislike mathematics, for it seems to have no meaning or relevance to their lives.

This book is for parents and teachers who want children to value mathematics and to experience the wonder of discovery. However, it is not the type of book that parents and teachers can give to their children as they might give a medicine, one measured dose at a time. Instead, *Children, Teachers, and Mathematics* is designed to inform parents and teachers, making them wiser and more insightful guides for developing children. It is a developmental and educational road map, pointing out a few of the more important junctions in the journey from childhood to adulthood, examining important issues, and suggesting ways to motivate and sustain the children's interest in mathematics.

David A. Thomas

CHILDREN,
TEACHERS, AND
MATHEMATICS

CHAPTER 1

The Mind of a Child

Who can gaze into the bright, expectant eyes of a child and not sense the wonder with which children greet their world? Parents and teachers should rejoice at that look, for it contains an invitation to join in an exploration of the world and of life itself. But what kind of mind is issuing the invitation, and which is the best way to learn?

This chapter examines these questions as they apply to children in the primary grades, their teachers, and their curriculum.

WHICH IS THE BEST WAY TO LEARN?

Talk to enough parents and educators and you will sense a basic disagreement over what ought to be taught in school and how best to do the teaching. The two sides in this debate often appear to be arguing for two radically different types of schooling: one highly structured and focused on skill acquisition and memorization of factual information, the other more interested in an exploration of the world and the

1

search for meaning. To understand the reasons behind this clash of opinions, you must first consider the theories of learning held by the two sides in this debate.

The Absorption Theory of Learning

In the absorption theory of learning (Baroody 1987), knowledge equals facts and facts are to be memorized. Information is poured into the child as if she or he were a "vessel to be filled." Thus, facts, procedures, and concepts are presented for storage in memory. As a result, the child plays no executive role, being essentially a passive receiver.

According to this model, a knowledgeable person is one with a generous store of facts, concepts, and procedures within easy reach, and learning involves associating facts and skills in a stimulus-response mode. For instance, if you ask a child, "How much is 5 plus 3?", the child searches his or her memory for an answer associated with this question—in this case the number 8. In this mode of operation, the question of what it means to add two numbers is irrelevant. The point of the question is to see if the child can make the correct association and thereby produce the correct answer.

The teacher's role is to shape the child's responses appropriately. The child's role in this activity is passive. Through practice, the association between the question and the desired response can be made stronger in memory, producing speed and accuracy of response, or fluency. Thus learning becomes a kind of copying process: the child memorizes a body of factual information and associations. Implicit in this model of learning are the assumptions that facts are stored in memory as discrete, snapshot-like images of the world, and that memory has separate storage bins for every fact we learn. In summary, this model requires the learner to play a passive role, concentrating on stimulus-response activities. Motivation for learning is provided by external rewards, since the act of learning itself offers little intrinsic reward.

Cognitive Theory of Learning

In cognitive theory (Baroody 1987), knowledge equals internal representations acquired through active analysis of data, sensory impressions, and so on. In other words, children create knowledge internally by building up their own model of the world. Since the child's analysis and interpretations constitute knowledge in this model, information "poured" into the child is meaningless in and of itself. A child is not so much a vessel to be filled as a "lamp to be lit"; the child's focus should be on an active search for meaning. A knowledgeable person is one who possesses insight, understands complex relationships, and can solve problems never before encountered.

In this model of learning, facts and concepts are not stored in memory as snapshots of the world. Rather, the model proposes that children identify the most significant features of a thought and the relationships between those features. This information is then stored. Later, when recall is required, this information is used to recreate the original thought. In this manner, vast amounts of information can be stored efficiently. This model also explains why memories become stronger as we realize more fully the relationships which explain the meaning of the thought. For instance, the facts $3 \times 1 = 3, 5 \times 1 = 5, 8 \times 1 = 8$ are more easily learned using the generalization that multiplication by 1 always returns the other factor as an answer. Similarly, as soon as a learner discovers that addition is commutative, the sums $3 + 2$ and $2 + 3$ can be treated as equivalent sums. Such discoveries greatly reduce the number of "facts" which must ultimately be mastered. Precisely this type of active discovery is the heart of "understanding" in the cognitive theory. Indeed, the learner's role is involved more with linking previously learned concepts to create new, more efficient insights than with the rote memorization of isolated facts.

Because children must, in this model, create their own understandings, one would expect them to develop thoughts and processes that are different from those employed by their teachers and parents. Naturally, these understandings may be "invisible" to the casual observer. For example, children in the primary grades use all kinds of interesting counting strategies to do arithmetic computations. The parent or teacher need only listen to the children as they "think out loud" to realize that they are using strategies involving finger counting, counting down, and other techniques long abandoned by the adult listener.

With respect to motivation, in the cognitive model, children's curiosity and need to make sense of the world become the driving force in their efforts. Because they are active participants in their own learning, the satisfactions of mastering a new concept or skill are intrinsically motivating. No external reward is necessary.

The Mathematics Our Children Will Need

Unless mankind destroys or abandons technology as a basis for modern civilization, mathematics will become more important in both professional and private life. At the same time, the centuries-old skills of paper-and-pencil computation will decrease in importance, replaced by the use of electronic computing devices, as greater importance is placed on analytic skills and mathematical problem solving. Where once every citizen needed to know how to use pencil and paper to do complex arithmetic operations involving fractions, decimals, and percents, the next generation of citizens will be expected to perform these calculations routinely in the context of sophisticated computer models and simulations. Consequently, the capacity to perform mathematical analyses and solve complex problems will become more important than the ability to recall mathematical facts or perform routine mathematical computations.

Parents and teachers wishing to encourage children to develop an analytical approach to mathematics may profit from considering the following suggestions. When you discuss mathematics or science with a child, point out relationships embedded in the concept or topic, and appreciate the insights discovered by the child. For instance, when discussing the features of a rectangle, measure the opposite sides, talk about the sides being parallel, note the four right angles, compare these features with those of a square. Do squares have the same features as rectangles? In what ways are they different? Are there any squares to be seen in a grocery store? And so on.

Another strategy for encouraging the development of mathematical insight is to examine concepts, processes, figures, etc. from more than one perspective. For instance, in discussing the meaning of multiplication, you might represent multiplication as:

1. repeated addition

$$3 * 4 = 4 + 4 + 4 \text{ or } XXXX + XXXX + XXXX$$

2. a rectangular array

$$3 \; * \; 4 \; = \; \begin{matrix} XXXX \\ XXXX \\ XXXX \end{matrix}$$

3. a 3-by-4 rectangle drawn on graph paper

When discussing subtraction, you might consider alternative methods of computation:

1. 5 − 3 means start at 5 and count backward 3 steps. The number you land on is the answer. (This might be done using a number line.)

2. 5 − 3 means start at the smaller number, 3, and count forward until you get to 5. The number of steps taken is the answer. (Do this on a number line as well.)

After discussing both methods of subtraction separately, comparisons may be discussed. Why do you get the same answer using both methods? Can you make up a story problem for each method to illustrate why the method is a valid way of computing the difference 5 − 3? Use toys or other manipulative objects to act out the story problem.

Mathematical discussions conducted in a relaxed and playful manner are intrinsically rewarding to children. Parents and teachers should share the enjoyment of these experiences and look for ways to make such discussions a routine part of life. These experiences give meaningful learning a chance to develop over time. However, children cannot discover mathematics on cue. A relaxed, supportive atmosphere is necessary, one that encourages reflection and repeated exposure to concepts. Also, always use a great deal of discussion (dialogue, not lecture) and a variety of concrete representations and manipulatives whenever your goal is concept development.

Two Priorities

According to the cognitive theory of learning, real comprehension in mathematics requires the learner to validate concepts first-hand. Genuine mathematical reasoning involves metacognition or executive processing of thinking. Until children are capable of this type of self-awareness, they are not really doing mathematics. Thus, the development of a meaningful basis for mathematics is the first priority in learning mathematics.

The second priority in mathematics is the development of confidence and fluency. Increased accuracy and speed on routine tasks free students to focus their attention on strategic, problem-solving thinking. Children and adults who must constantly double-check every aspect of their work rarely become sophisticated problem-solvers. Therefore, students must develop speed and accuracy. The drill and practice methods of the absorption theory are appropriate for developing fluency with math facts and other routine tasks.

A reasonable approach to teaching mathematics is to recognize the merits of both theories of learning and use each wisely: a cognitive approach for concept development and problem solving; a stimulus-response (absorption) approach to develop speed and accuracy.

However, knowing which approach to use involves more than an appreciation of mathematics. Teachers and parents need to appreciate the special needs of young learners. Two-month-old minds have their own priorities, largely relating to the oral investigation of fingers, toes, and loose objects within reach. Two-year-old minds play with language and roam through the house and back yard in search of things to see, touch, and possibly (still) eat. As children grow, their interests change; their abilities change; their needs change. Understanding these developmental changes is an important key to understanding the needs of children of different ages.

THE WORK OF JEAN PIAGET

Among the many researchers who have studied and written about child development, few have had as profound an effect on the thinking of American mathematics educators as the Swiss philosopher Jean Piaget (1896–1980). For over sixty years, Piaget studied the natural emergence and development of logical thinking in children and published his findings in numerous books and articles. Although Piaget never claimed that his theory had anything to do with teaching or school curricula, his many interpreters see a connection.

Since the emergence and development of logical thinking in children is not directly observable, they must be observed indirectly in the course of discussions and problem-solving activities. Consequently, Piaget's experiments and observations frequently asked children to make mathematical concepts and processes the focus of their attention. In these situations, the researchers' focus was not on teaching mathematics but rather on observing the child's ability to think logically about isolated mathematical concepts and problems. Basically, Piaget's research examined the question, "What logical tools do children bring to the study of mathematics?" This is a question of child development. On the other hand, mathematics educators are typically more interested in the questions, "What do children need to know?" and "How should they be taught?" These are questions of curriculum and instruction. Clearly, the questions are related, but not the same.

As a result of his studies, Piaget concluded that the development of logical thinking in children occurs in stages. Many of his interpreters concluded that mathematics learning also occurs in the same stages. Gradually, this idea has been accepted by many scholars, publishers, teachers, administrators, and curriculum planners across the nation. As a result, these professionals have rewritten much of the elementary school mathematics curriculum and changed the way that mathematics is taught in America.

Stages of Intellectual Development

According to Piaget's (and his interpreters) theory, normal intellectual growth is not a continuous process. Instead, new talents and capabilities are acquired in biologically-timed surges that occur every few years. The observable results of these changes include new interests, new insights, and more sophisticated reasoning. At the same time, the child acquires other abilities that are not announced immediately by new behaviors. Such abilities may remain hidden until the day the child attempts some new trick or task and finds that he or she can actually do it.

Significant new behaviors announce to the outside world the beginning of a new stage of intellectual development in the child. At different stages, these new behaviors may take on a variety of forms: the first signs of intentional behavior, in which a child actively seeks for lost toys or favorite foods; a sudden attempt at explaining things using cause-and-effect reasoning; the beginnings of abstract thought; and so on. Piaget's names for these stages are sensorimotor, preoperational, concrete operations, and formal operations (see Table 1.1).

In Piagetian theory, after the onset of each new stage, little if any new potential arises for several years. This is not wasted time; during these years, a child learns to make use of his or her new abilities, applying them to the perfection of new skills and the development of new concepts. Parents and teachers interested in helping children make use of their new abilities need only be observant to notice new behaviors. Listen to the children. Watch them. In their speech and play, you will see hints of new talents and interests. Activities based on these emerging natural interests are almost always good choices.

On the other hand, parents ambitious for the success of their children should note that encouragement and educational enrichment, although helpful, probably cannot accelerate their children's development in the sense of endowing the children with abilities beyond their years. Well-intentioned efforts must always take into consideration a child's present stage of development and seek to select activities appropriate to the child's present abilities. Enrichment activities should always be selected as a means of developing a child's existing potential. Children pressed to perform beyond their ability can be frustrated and discouraged and, ultimately, "turned off" to learning.

The educational implications of the first three stages of Piaget's four-stage model of intellectual development are discussed below. The final stage, formal operations, is discussed in Chapter 2. Because this book is about the development of mathematical thinking in school children, comments describing the stages are basically limited to the child's mathematical thinking or to behaviors that are thought to be related to the development of mathematical thinking. To say everything about all aspects of child development at any given stage would be beyond the scope and intention of this book. Also, approximate ages are indicated, but should not be regarded as absolute. Each child has

Table 1.1 Piaget's Stages of Intellectual Development

Approximate Ages	Stages
Birth–two	Sensorimotor
Two–six	Preoperational
Six–twelve	Concrete operations
Twelve through adulthood	Formal operations

his or her own schedule; parents and teachers should harken to that schedule.

Sensorimotor Stage: Birth to Age Two

From birth, and possibly even before, babies seem to be listening to their world. Newborn babies have been observed to turn their heads in response to sounds, in a way that suggests that the language-processing centers of their brains are beginning the search for meaning. Older babies are also aware of changes in their surroundings and apparently are interested in variety in visual stimulation.

Since babies are believed to profit from a rich variety of visual and auditory stimulation, parents should give some thought to providing their infants with bright, cheerful surroundings that offer music, talk, and other routine sounds of life. Naturally, a child can be tired by too much stimulation, and parents ought always to be sure that the objects used pose no threat. With these cautions in mind, parents can experiment with visual and auditory stimuli for their infants.

As nature takes its course, children become more active in exploring their environment. They show intent by actively seeking out objects, grasping and crawling to reach them. After gaining some use of hands, arms, and legs, children begin purposeful explorations, moving about the floor of the house, searching out interesting objects, and developing the rudiments of language.

During this stage, children are interested in seeing, touching, and tasting almost everything within reach. If safe, colorful blocks of different shapes and sizes are provided, these objects will generally interest the child and may provide a natural focus for the development of language. For example, children near the end of this stage of development, who have started talking in brief sentences, might indicate that they want a BIG cookie, not a SMALL cookie, or a ROUND cookie, not a SQUARE cookie. Parents may introduce their children to such terminology without fear. Simply observe whether the child picks up the word and uses it voluntarily. If the child rejects the use of the word, relax, as it can be mastered at a later stage.

Preoperational Stage: Ages Two to Six

Among the many developmental tasks appropriate to this stage, one of the most important is the mastery of oral language. During these years, children must learn to listen attentively, ask pertinent questions, and express themselves clearly. For parents interested in fostering the development of oral language and critical thinking, the best recommendation is to read to your child every day. Find stories he or she enjoys, and read them with feeling. Encourage your child to express his or her expectations regarding the outcome of the story. For example, "What do you think will happen when the big, bad wolf tries to blow down the house made of bricks?" Talk about the characters: "How do you feel about the wolf in the story? Is he like anyone you know?" Share in the excitement and the satisfaction. Ask why the characters feel and act the way they do. Share your own feelings: "I'm really enjoying this story. Are you?" Your child will cherish the time spent in this manner and develop positive attitudes toward reading and the habit of thinking about what is being read. Children who begin school with this background frequently become excellent readers and successful students in general. Remember—the object is not to teach your child to read or to lecture him or her; the point is to have fun while you share a story.

In addition to reading aloud, parents and preschool teachers can encourage children in the development of language by talking with the child (not *at* the child) every day about shared experiences and activities. Some of us grew up in homes in which the parents did the talking and the children did only the listening. If you grew up in that type of home, you may experience some uneasiness with this suggestion, but consider the payoff if you can learn to talk with your child. First of all, you will start to discover what is going on in his or her head and heart. Second, your child will discover what *you* think. Third, in sharing your thoughts, your child will learn to carry on a discussion and take pleasure in it. All these discoveries are of enormous importance to children.

So make cookies, plant flower seeds for a window box, make collections, play games, and so on, all the time discussing your mutual thoughts and feelings. If you share the child's thoughts in this manner, you will begin to recognize some of the following general characteristics typical of children at the preoperational stage of development.

CHARACTERISTIC BEHAVIORS According to Piaget's theory, preoperational children are egocentric. They think everything exists for their own use and benefit. This characteristic often troubles parents, who equate such behavior with adult selfishness. However, there is an important difference between the egocentricism of a preoperational child and that of an adult. In a preoperational child, the capacity to put himself or herself in another's position or to see a problem from another's perspective may not yet have developed. One assumes that adults acting selfishly have made an informed choice to behave in such a manner. To a child not capable of even understanding the choice, parental anger over "selfish" behavior must seem both incomprehensible and unjust. To avoid an unfortunate reaction in such moments, parents would be well-advised to question the child carefully so as to determine his or her understanding of the situation.

Preoperational children are also perception-bound, which means that they are more apt to reach a conclusion based on the way something looks than on reasoning. For instance, even after counting both rows of *'s in Figure 1.1, a child at this stage will insist that there are more *'s in the top row than in the bottom row.

The dominant role that perception plays in a child's thinking may be demonstrated in another simple test. Take some clay and roll it into a cigar shape. Then roll it into a ball. Ask a preoperational child to compare the amount of clay in the ball with the amount of clay in the cigar shape. In most cases, preoperational children will say that there is more clay in the cigar shape than in the ball. The notion that the amount of clay is unchanged by the way it is shaped is alien to preoperational children, because they cannot reverse their thinking and mentally transform the cigar into the ball and back again.

The same lack of reversible thinking can be seen in other types of situations. For instance, the following sequence of questions and answers typifies the child's inability to put himself in another's position or reverse his thinking.

Adult to boy: "Do you have a brother?"

Boy: "No."

Adult to boy: "Does your sister have a brother?"

Boy: "No."

```
*     *     *     *     *
   *   *   *   *   *
```

**FIGURE 1.1   Are There More *'s
in the Top Row?**

Preoperational children do not do part-whole thinking well. For instance, if a preschool child is asked to decide whether a cocker spaniel is both a dog and a mammal, or whether a mallard is both a duck and a bird, the child is apt to perceive the choice as improper even if he or she appears to understand what mammals and birds are. In most cases, the child would reject one category and select the other. To the preoperational child, the cocker spaniel must belong to one category or the other, since part-whole relationships are not part of his or her thinking. The thoughts "All ducks are birds" and "All dogs are mammals" would be alien to a typical preoperational child because the meanings of "all" and "some" are not yet established in his or her mind.

On the other hand, the acquisition of this type of thinking must rank as one of the most significant achievements of a preschooler, with profound implications once formal education begins. Therefore, parents and preschool teachers should be alert for opportunities to help children develop the use of this concept, once they are ready for it. Sorting activities based on familiar objects should form the setting for such development. Later in this book, a number of activities using attribute materials are presented to address the development of part-whole thinking.

When dealing with a complex sorting situation, preoperational children cannot focus on more than one feature at a time. Young children learn to sort things first by shape, then by color, and finally by size (Copeland 1984). Later on, around five or six years of age, they are able to sort things on the basis of any of these three criteria. For instance, they can sort a pile of toys on the basis of color. However, when more than one attribute must be used in the sorting, they cannot simultaneously sort into the following four piles: red animals; animals that are not red; red toys that are not animals; toys that are not red and are not animals.

INFORMAL MATHEMATICAL THINKING During the preschool years, most children engaged in activities involving numbers focus on counting and quantity-comparison activities. For example, children might count the number of cookies on a plate, the number of flowers growing in a window box, and so forth. When they use counting to compare two quantities, they may be demonstrating a concern for the fairness of some division of wealth, such as candies or gifts.

By the time children enter school, most have developed an understanding of numbers that is analogous to a kind of number line (Figure

1.2). This concept, which they bring to school, allows them to count and compare quantities. However, this is true only for small quantities. A typical child might know his numbers from one to twenty upon entering school. Also, many children have trouble starting a count sequence with any number other than one.

Concrete Operational Stage: Ages Six to Twelve

In Piaget's model, this stage marks the beginning of logical, mathematical reasoning. It is also the stage of intellectual development at which a child is generally ready to start the first grade. A preoperational child may not compete well or cooperate easily with his concrete operational classmates in many areas of the first grade curriculum. For this reason, parents should take seriously the advice of kindergarten teachers who think that a child may not be ready for first grade. Many children who were placed in the first grade a year too soon have had to play "catch up" during the rest of their education. Most such children never do quite catch up, because the instruction they receive is always a little too advanced for their development.

CHARACTERISTIC BEHAVIORS What are some of the characteristics of concrete operational children? Unlike a preoperational child who still makes decisions based on the way things look, a concrete operational child will use logic to reach a decision. The following demonstration illustrates the difference between the two types of thinking.

With a preoperational and a concrete operational child watching, select three glasses and place them side by side on a table. One glass should be tall and slender, and the other two glasses should be identical, both shorter and wider than the first glass. Fill the identical, shorter glasses half full of water so the water levels are the same. Then pour the contents of one of the shorter glasses into the taller glass. Place the two glasses containing water side by side on the table and ask each child to make a statement about the amount of water in each glass.

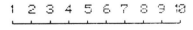

FIGURE 1.2 Number Line

A typical concrete operational child will reach the logical conclusion that the amounts of water must be the same, even if they do not look the same. The preoperational child cannot make that choice or accept it. The appearance of the taller column of water is overpowering evidence for the preoperational child. Even if the contents of the taller glass are poured back into the other short glass and the liquid levels compared and found equal, the preoperational child will probably insist that there was more water in the taller glass.

THE MEANING OF "CONCRETE"   A second important feature of thinkers in this category is implied in the name "concrete operational." Children at this stage of development can reason logically about things they have experienced, as opposed to unfamiliar or hypothetical situations. One way to experience a mathematical problem is to model the conditions and procedures described in the problem by using manipulative objects.

A man has three cats. His friend gives him two more cats. How many cats does he have then?

In solving this problem, a concrete operational child would first select some set of objects to represent the cats, then model the problem by manipulating the objects in the set to recreate the events described in the word problem. For example, using beans as cats, the child might count out three beans and place them in a pile representing the original three cats. Next, the child would count out two more beans, adding them to the first pile. Finally, the child would count the number of beans in the pile to get the answer.

The merits of this approach from the child's point of view are substantial. First, only one number need be considered at a time. Although concrete operational children can consider more than one attribute of a single object at a time and understand part-whole relationships, they find it difficult to consider two different objects or processes at the same time. Using a manipulative model, each part of the problem can be addressed separately, and intermediate results saved physically (rather than saved in memory) for later use.

Second, the model embodies both the original problem and the child's thinking about how to attack and solve the problem. Once again, because the child can focus on only one aspect of any given problem at a time, he or she cannot simultaneously both solve a problem and critically examine his or her thinking for flaws. The use of manipulatives enables the child to solve a problem and record both thinking and results by use of the concrete materials. After obtaining a solution to the problem, the child may then go back and see if his or her thinking was reasonable.

Third, children often find it easier to show a person what they did than to describe what they were thinking. For example, if children need to share their thoughts with a classmate or explain them to the teacher, it may be easier to reenact the strategy used than to say what happened. Children can get tongue-tied and frustrated in trying to describe actions which did not require speech.

THE IMPORTANCE OF PART-WHOLE THINKING   One of the most important tasks of early primary school children is the application of part-whole thinking to problems concerning quantity. Part-whole thinking typically is applied to triples of numbers.

Jim has two marbles and John gives him three more. How many does Jim have now?

The numbers two and three in this problem are treated by most adults as parts that, when combined, produce the whole (five) sought in the problem statement. In solving this type of problem, many parents and teachers use part-whole thinking without realizing it. This can have significant consequences when a parent or teacher tries to help a struggling child. Without realizing it, most people use part-whole thinking to select a problem-solving strategy: whether to add, subtract, multiply, or divide the two numbers given in the problem. If a parent or teacher is not able to reveal this selection process to children and so appears somehow to make the correct choice of operation based on insight, children can easily conclude that they do not have that type of insight and never will.

To help children really understand this type of word problem, parents and teachers must teach them to interpret word problems in light of the part-whole concept. That is, in reading the problem, children must determine whether each number given is a part or the whole. If the whole is given, then a part must be the quantity sought after. Parts are generally found by using subtraction in some form. On the other hand, if the whole is the sought-after quantity, addition is usually used.

To help you practice this concept, read each of the following problems (David 1983) and identify which numbers are parts, which number is the whole, and whether the quantity you are looking for is a part or a whole.

Change problems:

- Joe has five marbles. Jim gives him three more. How many does Joe have now?

- Joe had six marbles. Jim gave him some more. Now he has ten marbles. How many did Jim give Joe?

Equalizing problems:

- Joe has seven marbles. Jim has ten. How many more does Joe need to have as many as Jim?

Combination problems:

- Joe has three marbles. Jim has six. How many do they have altogether?

- Joe and Jim have nine marbles. Joe has seven. How many does Jim have?

Comparison problem:

- Joe has seven marbles. Jim has nine. How many more does Jim have than Joe?

Using the part-whole concept, the meaning of addition and subtraction can be considered simultaneously. This is a more natural approach to learning mathematics than the traditional one of teaching addition and then subtraction. Using concrete manipulatives and the part-whole concept, children can learn the meaning of these operations simultaneously and begin to realize that in some sense, addition and subtraction are opposites of one another. This realization will pay off later as the child struggles to master the large body of math facts taught in the primary grades. For instance, to the child who understands both addition and subtraction, and who also recognizes their relationship, the following math facts are related, not completely separate.

$$2 + 3 = 5 \qquad 3 + 2 = 5$$
$$5 - 2 = 3 \qquad 5 - 3 = 2$$

By recognizing these relationships, the child can reduce the number of separate facts to be memorized. Relationships like these also give the child a means to verify or check uncertain "facts."

INFORMAL MATHEMATICAL THINKING Children commonly develop mental computational strategies by incorporating the part-whole concept and counting strategies to solve many routine problems.

> **Mary has five candies. Sue gives her three more. How many does Mary have in all?**

In solving this problem, a child is apt to use a very different strategy than an adult would. The child might begin by setting a mental "internal counter" to five candies, then "add on" three more, using an ordinal (counting) sense of number. After adding on the necessary three words ("six, seven, eight"), the child stops counting at eight and identifies this as the answer. By contrast, adults are more apt to rely on memorized math facts or associations with similar problems solved previously.

Children sometimes do subtraction problems by counting backward a specified number of steps from an initial value. For example, some children solve the problem 7 − 3 by mentally counting backwards three numbers ("six, five, four") and identifying the number they land on as the answer. Another method is to set the internal counter at the smaller of the two numbers, then count up to the larger number, keeping track with their fingers ("four, five, six, seven"). The answer is the number of fingers used (in this case, four). Naturally, children are capable of using both methods if they understand both, choosing the speedier option where possible.

Parents and teachers can help children become more versatile and competent problem-solvers by following a simple principle: *It is better to solve one problem two ways than two problems the same way.*

That is, after a thorough discussion of a problem and an evaluation of the strategy used in solving it, try to think of a second way to do the problem. Look for an alternative point of view or a fact or concept not used in the first solution. By spending this extra time, you promote one of the most important qualities of great problem-solvers: You are more interested in the problem itself and the opportunities it presents for mathematical thinking than you are in any particular solution. This habit, practiced over years of development, can bloom into an independent mind capable of critical thought, one of education's finest products.

A Few Cautions

Piaget's theory offers mathematics educators a relatively simple, top-down, conceptual model for the development of logical thinking in children. Although the theory focuses on the development of logical behaviors, rather than on the development of mathematical concepts and skills, it does provide a helpful tool with which to think about some of the complex issues of mathematics learning. In particular, Piaget's model makes it easier to think about questions such as "Is my child ready for first grade mathematics?" The theory offers little help on questions such as "What is a child really thinking while doing arithmetic?"

The real problem with using Piaget's model as a tool for researching mathematics learning is the tremendous "gap between Piaget's tasks and the tasks of school mathematics" (Groen & Kieran 1983). While providing insight into the development of logical thought, Piaget's theory does not provide a detailed explanation of how children actually use logic while doing mathematics. For this reason, caution should be used when Piaget's name is invoked in support of a specific curricular or instructional change. Other perspectives should also be considered, particularly if the research base on which they are founded explains how children actually use logic while doing mathematics. The information-processing approach provides just such a perspective.

THE INFORMATION-PROCESSING APPROACH

If Piaget's theory and its various interpretations offer a broad view of logical thinking without much detail, the information-processing approach offers just the opposite: detail without a strong theory. Although the information-processing approach has not yet developed a comprehensive theory of its own, some findings based on this approach challenge the validity of Piaget's theory of intellectual development. In spite of such disagreements over theory, by examining the processes that children use in solving mathematics problems, researchers have learned much that is relevant to curricular and instructional issues.

Information-processing research usually involves one or more of the following approaches: individual, in-depth interviews with children; analysis of error patterns; response latencies (Carpenter and Moser 1983).

In the first approach (David 1983), students are assigned a mathematical task to perform in the presence of an interviewer and one or more observers. As the student proceeds with the task, his or her actions are recorded by the observers and may be videotaped. The interviewer asks questions and gives hints, according to a strictly defined, predetermined role. The purpose of each such task-based interview is to identify what the student is thinking while addressing the task. The student may be asked to think out loud while doing the problem, relating any insights, remembered facts, and attempted calculations. Studies of this type reveal a great deal about the actual thinking processes used by children.

The second approach, error-pattern analysis, examines the systematic errors made by children as they attempt to solve sets of problems. If a particular type of problem generates characteristic errors, inferences may be made concerning the nature of children's procedural or strategic thinking. This approach often provides valuable information when the tasks are easily defined. If tasks are complex, as in the case of word problems, this approach tends to fail.

The third approach, response latencies, also avoids the self-reporting and observation of task-based interviews. In this approach, a data base of information is developed that describes the time required for a student to complete each of a set of simple, discrete tasks. Once this information is available for a given student, a more complex task is presented, requiring the strategic use of several simple tasks in sequence. By comparing the overall time spent solving the complex task with the times required for all the simple tasks, an inference may be made regarding which of the simple tasks were employed.

Studies based on these and other information-processing approaches have provided mathematics educators with important information about what children know and how they think. This, in turn, informs our decisions about what teachers need to know about children and how mathematics ought to be taught. Kaplan, Yamamoto, and Ginsburg (1989) state that teachers need the ability to see mathematics through their students' eyes and that this ability consists (at least) of:

- Knowledge of children's typical interpretations of questions, instructions, procedures, and a vocabulary of school mathematics at all levels;
- Knowledge of individual children's unique interpretations of these topics;
- Knowledge about how to introduce formal mathematics by building on children's existing abilities, by helping children to generalize informal knowledge of new and abstract situations, and by encouraging the formation of connections between what children already know and the abstract representations of mathematics.

These recommendations imply that mathematics educators' knowledge of child development must go far beyond the general notions of Piaget's stages. Unfortunately, the detailed knowledge required by the recommendations is not yet complete, nor is it likely to be for decades. Nevertheless, enough is known to start improving the quality of instruction in several areas of the mathematics curriculum.

TEACHING FOR MEANING: TWO EXAMPLES

Mathematics education in the primary grades must address a number of objectives (see chapter 3), using teaching strategies that appeal to children, stress meaning, and promote the development of appropriate beliefs about mathematics and students' role in learning mathematics. The following examples illustrate an approach to teaching that emphasizes concept and language development.

Decimal Numeration

Just as part-whole thinking is critical in problem solving, the concept of decimal numeration (base-ten place values) is critical in the mastery of pencil-and-paper computation during the primary years. Normally, decimal numeration is introduced formally about the second grade. Addition and subtraction involving "carrying" and "borrowing" represent the first major applications of this concept.

A number of ways can be used to introduce children to decimal numeration. One good way involves the use of a set of concrete manipulatives called numeration materials (Figure 1.3). Briefly, these materials consist of the following objects:

Chips (Squares 1 centimeter on a side). Prepare fifty of these, using a paper cutter and centimeter graph paper.

Strips (Rectangles 1 centimeter by 10 centimeters). Ten chips should be clearly drawn on each strip. Prepare thirty of these, using a paper cutter and centimeter graph paper.

Flats (Squares 10 centimeters on a side). One hundred chips should be clearly drawn on each flat. Prepare nine flats, using a paper cutter and centimeter graph paper.

Using these materials, parents, teachers, and students can represent whole numbers from 1 to 999. Digits in the hundreds column are represented by using flats; digits in the tens column are represented by using strips; and digits in the ones column are represented by using chips. For example, the number 524 would be represented using five flats, two strips, and four chips. These objects should be arranged in columns corresponding to hundreds, tens, and ones, from left to right, observing the rule, "No more than nine chips may occupy the ones

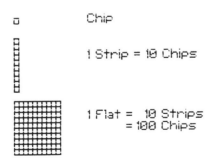

FIGURE 1.3   Numeration
Materials

column; no more than nine strips may occupy the tens column; and so on."

In studying numeration, care should be taken to include plenty of practice with each form of the number: the concrete representation using the chips, strips, and flats; the abstract written form (524); and the spoken form (five hundred and twenty-four). Children need to practice moving back and forth between these representations until they can do so smoothly and without effort.

Once a child can represent numbers in all three forms, she or he is ready to deal meaningfully with addition and subtraction algorithms (procedures). Everyone studied these in elementary school. However, as many readers may recall, the procedures were not always learned correctly. Mistakes were made, particularly when it came to "carrying" and "borrowing." Today, these troublesome activities are lumped together by mathematics teachers under the term "regrouping."

When children make mistakes in addition and subtraction problems that require regrouping, they are often following incorrect or incomplete algorithms. Children invent erroneous procedures and use them without any reference to the meanings of the place values in the numbers. That is, they ignore numeration. This allows them to make a galaxy of mistakes. Children using such home-grown algorithms typically fail to recognize the flaws in their thinking. Often, students who do realize they have a problem merely embellish their incorrect algorithm with some additional, flawed flourishes in the hopes of arriving at an acceptable answer.

In light of this trait, it is imperative that children develop knowledge structures that refer back to the meaning of addition, subtraction, and numeration, and can use these structures when faced with doubt. In this way, using concrete models to capture the meaning and work out their strategies, children can evaluate the merit of their ideas and attempts at problem solving and know when they are wrong.

The following examples illustrate how the use of numeration materials provides a meaningful way to learn addition and subtraction with regrouping. Prior to using the numeration materials in this manner, children should practice exchanging ten chips for one strip, one strip for ten chips, one flat for ten strips, and so on.

Figure 1.4 begins in the upper left hand corner with the indicated sum 27 + 4 written in vertical form. A light line is used to separate the digits in the units column from the digits in the tens column. To the right of this, chips and strips have been used to represent the original problem. Notice that the chips in the ones column of the answer row are arranged so that ten chips appear in one column and the remaining chip in a separate column. Referring to the rule that states, "No more than nine chips may remain in the ones column," the student exchanges the ten chips for a strip and places this "carry" in the tens column. Finally, having made all necessary regroupings, the sum is tallied in each column and the answer 31 obtained.

Children should practice problems of this sort until they consistently obtain the correct answers and have confidence that they understand the algorithm. When this has been achieved, addition problems involving the conversion of strips into flats may also be attempted, such as 27 + 84. When more than nine strips are found in the tens column, groups of ten strips must be converted to flats, and the flats transferred to the hundreds column.

The concept of borrowing by using numeration materials is illustrated in Figure 1.5. Once again, the original problem 23 − 6 is first written in vertical form. Next, strips and chips are used to represent the problem. In this case, the number on the bottom row represents the number of chips and/or strips that must be removed from the top

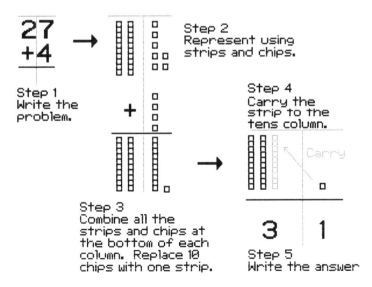

FIGURE 1.4   Addition with Regrouping

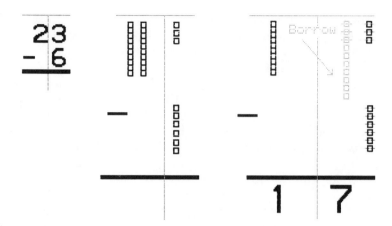

FIGURE 1.5   Subtraction with Regrouping

row. Since there are not enough chips in the ones column of the top row to allow seven to be removed, the child converts one strip to ten chips and places the chips in the ones column. Finally, the subtraction is performed and the result 17 obtained.

Eventually, children will abandon the strips and chips, having mastered the meaning of the algorithm. Such children are less apt to carry in the wrong direction or borrow from the wrong column when using standard algorithms, because they understand what those actions mean.

Multiplication of Whole Numbers

Although several ways may be used to model the concept of multiplication, most children find the concept of repeated addition the easiest to understand. For example, the indicated sum 8 + 8 + 8 is readily accepted as three "eights" by most children. This language is easily modified to the form "three times eight," supporting a natural transfer from the concept and language of addition to the concept and language of multiplication. Once this modification is understood, children should be encouraged to use the new concept and new language to describe the world around them. For instance, in a group of five students, the question might be asked, "How many shoes are there?" Using repeated addition, the answer could be represented as

$$2 \ + \ 2 \ + \ 2 \ + \ 2 \ + \ 2 \ = \ 10$$

Restating this by using the language of multiplication, a student might say, "Five groups of two equals ten, so five times two equals ten." Another student might then answer the question, "How many toes are in this group?" by using repeated addition:

$$10 \ + \ 10 \ + \ 10 \ + \ 10 \ + \ 10 \ = \ 50$$

or by saying, "Five groups of ten equals fifty, so five times ten equals fifty."

The goal of this activity is to promote the simultaneous development of a meaningful concept of multiplication, a language for multiplication, and a mathematical notation for multiplication. It is not enough for children to recognize the notation 3×2 as a multiplication problem calling for a numerical answer. They must also be able to interpret the notation linguistically as "three groups of two" and imagine some situation in which three groups of two would have some meaning, such as the number of ears in a group of three children.

While students are mastering the concept of multiplication as repeated addition, a geometrical basis for the concept can be provided as well. For example, Figure 1.6 shows several indicated products and

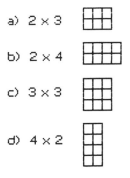

a) 2 × 3

b) 2 × 4

c) 3 × 3

d) 4 × 2

FIGURE 1.6   **Geometric Model for Multiplication**

their corresponding representations as rectangular arrays of squares. The first representation shows two rows of three squares, the second representation shows two rows of four, and so on. Students should develop fluency in the use of this concept and its language. Given an array, they should be able to describe it using the "*A* rows of *B*" terminology and represent it as the indicated product $A \times B$. Conversely, given an indicated product $A \times B$, they should be able to draw an array that represents the product. The point is to develop fluency in the use of the concept and its spoken and written representations.

In addition to developing single-digit multiplication, the rectangular array model of multiplication also provides a useful vehicle for discussing the numeration issues in two- and three-digit multiplication. Figure 1.7 illustrates this approach in the case of the product 23 × 32. The steps in creating the figure are as follows:

1. Using a sheet of graph paper, outline a rectangle 23 units tall and 32 units wide.

2. Draw horizontal lines through the rectangle every ten rows from the top edge. When fewer than ten rows remain, draw a horizontal line through the rectangle at every row.

3. Draw vertical lines through the rectangle every ten columns from the left edge. When fewer than ten columns remain, draw a vertical line through the rectangle at every column.

The original 23 × 32 rectangle has now been partitioned into the flats, strips, and chips of numeration materials: 6 flats; a group of 4

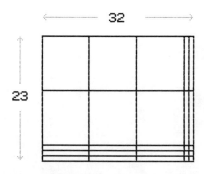

**FIGURE 1.7   Numeration Model
for Multiplication**

strips and a group of 9 strips, or 13 strips in all; and 6 chips. The product of 23 × 32 must therefore equal the sum of 600 + 130 + 6, or 736. Bridging the gap from this insight to the multiplication algorithm may be accomplished as follows:

First, review the numeration of two-digit and three-digit numbers by using flats, strips, and chips. Point out the fact that 23 and 32 may be written

$$23 = 20 + 3 \quad \text{and} \quad 32 = 30 + 2$$

Second, explain that the following two notations both indicate the product 23 × 32.

$$\begin{array}{c} 32 \\ \times\ 23 \end{array} \quad \text{may be written as} \quad \begin{array}{c} 30 + 2 \\ \times\ 20 + 3 \end{array}$$

Third, explain that the second notation indicates four products:

$$
\begin{aligned}
3 \times 2 &= 6 \\
3 \times 30 &= 90 \\
20 \times 2 &= 40 \\
20 \times 30 &= 600
\end{aligned}
$$

Fourth, note that each of these partial products is clearly associated with some part of the object in Figure 1.7.

$$
\begin{array}{rl}
30 + 2 & \{\textbf{width}\} \\
\times\ 20 + 3 & \{\textbf{height}\} \\
\hline
6 & \{\textbf{chips}\} \\
+\quad 90 & \{\textbf{horizontal strips}\} \\
+\quad 40 & \{\textbf{vertical strips}\} \\
+\quad 600 & \{\textbf{flats}\} \\
\hline
736 &
\end{array}
$$

Using this approach, the multiplication algorithm may be taken apart to reveal a meaningful sum of partial products associated with a rectangular array, all without having to "carry" digits from one column to another.

Once students understand what the partial products mean in such problems, the notation may be revised to take advantage of this understanding, and a conceptual bridge may be made to the conventional algorithm.

```
        52                              52
      × 27                            × 27
        14      {14 + 350}            364
   +   350
   +    40      {40 + 1000}        + 1040
   + 1000                            1404
     1404
```

Students who learn two-digit multiplication in this manner will have a meaningful concept of what multiplication means and why the multiplication algorithm works.

SUMMARY

Piaget's model of intellectual development offers teachers a conceptual tool for thinking about the emergence of logical thinking in children. Although Piaget himself never claimed that his theory had anything to say about formal schooling, his idea that children in the primary grades need to discover the meaning of mathematics through personal experience is now widely accepted. Recent information-processing research has cast doubt on the validity of Piaget's stages. Thus, Piaget's notion of stages will probably not influence researchers and curriculum specialists as it has in the past. However, by recognizing the characteristic talents and needs of concrete operational students, mathematics teachers are more likely to nurture primary students' natural interest in mathematics and support the development of each child's self-concept with regard to mathematics. By regarding each child first of all as a "lamp to be lit," and only secondarily as a "vessel to be filled," teachers at every level may build student confidence and foster an appreciation for mathematics.

DISCUSSION QUESTIONS

1. Do you agree or disagree with the following statement?

   Children in the primary grades live lives that are activity-oriented as opposed to lives that are reflective and passive.

> **Therefore, primary school mathematics ought to be activity-oriented.**

How would you support or challenge the statement if called on to do so at a faculty meeting?

2. What behavior might you look for as an indication that a child is using concrete manipulative materials productively?

3. In addition to paper and pencil, doing mathematics in a social setting like a school requires the development of certain specialized language skills. What specialized language skills does a child need for doing mathematics and how might you foster the development of those skills?

4. Is a child a "vessel to be filled" or a "lamp to be lit" in your school? Do you think that this issue has any importance at the secondary level? At the college level? At the postgraduate and professional level? Why?

5. Ask several children in primary grades to show you how they do problems involving part-whole thinking. What strategies are they using that you have never heard of or even imagined? If the strategies are sound but unconventional, do you think that the students should be encouraged to abandon their methods in favor of more common strategies? Why or why not?

6. What mathematical concepts and/or topics do you think are appropriate for kindergarten students? Do you think they should get a start on their math facts? Why or why not?

SUGGESTED READING AND REFERENCES

Baroody, Arthur J. *Children's Mathematical Thinking.* New York: Teachers College Press, 1987.

Carpenter, Thomas P., and James M. Moser. "The Acquisition of Addition and Subtraction Concepts." In *Acquisition of Mathematics Concepts and Processes,* edited by Richard Lesh and Marsha Landau. New York: Academic Press, 1983.

Copeland, Richard W. *How Children Learn Mathematics,* 4th ed. New York: Macmillan, 1984.

David, Robert B. "Complex Mathematical Cognition." In *The Development of Mathematical Thinking,* edited by Herbert P. Ginsburg. New York: Academic Press, 1983.

Groen, Guy, and Carolyn Kieran. "In Search of Piagetian Mathematics." In *The Development of Mathematical Thinking,* edited by Herbert P. Ginsburg. New York: Academic Press, 1983.

Kaplan, Rochelle G., Takashi Yamamoto, and Herbert P. Ginsburg. "Teaching Mathematics Concepts." In *Toward the Thinking Curriculum: Current Cognitive Research,* edited by Lauren B. Resnick, and Leopold E. Klopfer. Alexandria, VA: Association for Supervision and Curriculum Development, 1989.

CHAPTER 2

The Middle Years: Grades Five through Eight

The fourth and fifth grades are, for many students, the last golden years of childhood. By the sixth grade, many children are well into puberty, their inner peace gone for years to come. Indeed, some parents trace their first gray hairs to the year their oldest child began junior high. Of course, it's a good thing that children don't turn gray under stress, or every teenager would enter high school with white hair!

What is behind the problems of these "middle years"? In most cases, the normal stresses that children experience are caused by a multitude of bodily, emotional, intellectual, and social changes for which they are unprepared. Some boys begin to develop broader shoulders and facial hair. Some girls start to develop more noticeable breasts and hips. These changes (or lack thereof) are clearly visible and invite both comment and questions from the children. Accompanying these visible changes, a host of invisible forces assail the adolescent. Hormones rush through the body at new and alarming levels and at unwelcome times, summoning unwelcome emotions and contributing to a general feeling that something is out of control. Small wonder that puberty leaves an indelible mark on our lives, both as children and as parents and teachers of adolescents.

According to Piaget, children at this age also experience a significant change in mental capacity. This spurt in brain growth normally takes place in girls around age eleven. Boys tend to experience the same change about a year later (Figure 2.1). The new intellectual possibilities that arise in consequence of this brain growth often advertise themselves in the form of new behaviors and interests. Piaget called this new state the "formal operations" stage of thinking.

FORMAL OPERATIONAL THINKERS

The formal operations stage introduces a number of characteristics not available to concrete operational thinkers. However, these new characteristics do not suddenly appear fully developed. Children acquire the new traits gradually. Typically, a child will address one task as a formal operational thinker, only to revert to a concrete modality when attacking another task. This is normal. Indeed, college freshmen may function as concrete operational thinkers on many mathematical tasks,

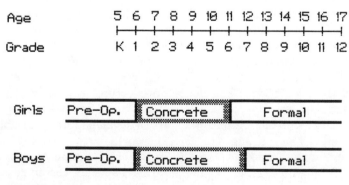

FIGURE 2.1   Brain Growth Chart

while dealing formally with problems encountered in other academic disciplines.

The following discussion presents the characteristics of formal operational thought, which should be kept in mind when pondering the goals of education.

Formal operational thinkers are deductive thinkers, recognizing cause and effect and formulating logical arguments. They use syllogistic reasoning: "All men are animals. Jim is a man. Therefore, Jim is an animal." Such thinkers are also metacognitive: They are aware of their own thinking processes and can evaluate that thinking critically. This capacity to evaluate arguments also makes it possible for them to see other points of view.

The capacity for critical thinking also has a significant impact on the imagination. Adolescents scorn childish imagination, preferring idealism and imaginative mental models. For instance, such people are capable of imagining a utopian society in great detail, paying serious attention to the abstractions upon which such models are built. Such thinkers are interested in concepts and pay close attention to generalizations and abstractions. They create theories to explain complex phenomena, think about abstractions, not just about concrete things and processes, and can reason about hypothetical situations not experienced in their own lives.

Mathematically, formal operational thinkers are different from concrete operational thinkers in that they use ratio and proportion to solve problems, understand and use probability in problem-solving situations and in the interpretation of data, and can conceptualize infinity. They also can create and use hierarchial classification schemes.

Finally, formal operational thinkers can question the ethical behavior of others and believe that authority is not a sufficient basis for determining ethical behavior.

Taken together, these characteristics describe a person capable of independent, abstract thought. They also describe a person who recognizes that the merits of an argument, theory, or conceptual model must be judged according to rigorous logical and experimental standards.

To the extent that children and adults fail to develop these characteristics, they fall short of several of education's most significant goals. Such people are also incapable of exercising all of their rights and responsibilities as citizens of a democracy. Therefore, in part, these characteristics represent not only facets of personal development, but desirable features of a self-governing electorate.

MATHEMATICS FOR THE MIDDLE GRADES

School mathematics in grades five through eight should reflect a growing concern for the relevance of mathematics to daily and professional life, and an awareness that children in these grades are developmentally ready for problem solving. This requires a mathematics curriculum that applies the concepts and computational skills developed in the primary grades to a wide variety of interesting real-life situations.

Some parents and teachers may argue that a focus on applications in grades five through eight is premature, because many students have not yet reached proficiency in pencil-and-paper arithmetic computations. A reaoned response to this concern is as follows. First, by retaining the focus of the mathematics curriculum on the concepts and skills presented in the primary grades, the students' new intellectual capabilities and interests are essentially ignored in favor of a rehash of the curriculum of the primary grades. Thus, an opportune moment may be lost and children may conclude that mathematics is a bore.

Second, there is little reason to believe that middle school students are any more ready to benefit from a study of arithmetic than they were as students in the primary grades. Indeed, there is every reason to believe that students are thoroughly bored by arithmetic by this time and are less likely than before to respond favorably to its study.

The third point is practical. Training in school ought to reflect the realities of life. From now on, arithmetic will be done using calculators and computers. Proficiency with paper-and-pencil computations is rapidly becoming a skill of questionable necessity, while proficiency with calculators and computers is becoming more and more critical. Also, it is clear that skill in mental estimation is an important companion skill to the use of calculating devices. A reasonable estimate is always a prudent backup to any answer obtained using a calculating device; after all, fingers do occasionally strike the wrong key.

Carried to the extreme, the concern for proficiency in paper-and-pencil computation has deadened the middle school mathematics curriculum. For instance, in seventh and eighth grade texts, only about

30 percent of the pages introduce any new material. The remaining 70 percent do nothing but review familiar topics. Even when teachers use texts that include chapters dealing with new material such as probability, statistics, geometry, and pre-algebra, they frequently skip those chapters because of "lack of time." No wonder fewer and fewer children rank mathematics among their favorite classes as they progress through elementary and junior high school.

Children in the middle grades are interested in the world, in life's challenges, and in their own ability to meet those challenges. For mathematics to have any value to such students, it must be relevant. One way to make mathematics relevant is to show how it may be used meaningfully in a wide range of situations and disciplines. Given the opportunity, students will become aware of the power of mathematics and their own capacity to solve real-world problems. What do students in your school district learn about mathematics in grades five through eight?

Middle school and lower secondary school mathematics texts tend to look alike in terms of topics, sequencing, use of graphics, exercises, and so on. Two exceptions to this general pattern are the Saxon series of texts and the University of Chicago School Mathematics Project (UCSMP) texts. This section briefly examines these two approaches to mathematics.

Saxon: One Man's Approach

When John Saxon, a former engineering instructor at the Air Force Academy, retired from the military and began teaching first-year algebra to junior college students, he developed and published an algebra text that implemented his own approach to teaching mathematics. The text, *Algebra 1: An Incremental Development* (Saxon 1981) is organized as 126 lessons and additional topics.

The text has no formal division of the 110 lessons and 16 additional topics into chapters. In Saxon's view, such divisions only interrupt the flow of learning. Also, compared to other major texts, more use of explanation and less use of illustrative graphics in the development of each lesson reflect Saxon's belief that an ongoing dialogue with plenty of examples is the best approach to instruction. However, perhaps the greatest difference lies in the use of exercises and problem sets.

Saxon's position on practice is that students need continual review of all they have learned. Thus, in every problem set, students are urged to do every problem, not just the odds or evens. Each set contains only a few items dealing with the new material in the current lesson. The remaining items systematically review previous lessons. This type of spaced, repeated practice, which only gradually assumes mastery of new material, is the heart of Saxon's approach.

This philosophy and format are repeated in Saxon's other texts. For example, in his junior high texts *Math 65: An Incremental Development* (1985) and *Math 76: An Incremental Development* (1987), Saxon says, "It is essential for students to work every problem in the lessons and in the problem set." With respect to use of calculators, Saxon states in the preface to *Math 76,* "We consider the use of calculators on the arithmetic level potentially debilitating. Until the use of calculators has been proved to produce positive results, we think it wise to avoid their use."

Saxon's claims regarding the effectiveness of his approach and texts are both supported and challenged by various researchers. Unfortunately, many studies investigating Saxon's materials do not meet rigorous standards of experimental design and control and must therefore be dismissed. One study that does meet such standards (Johnson 1987) found that although teachers and students appeared to like the Saxon texts better than a popular, conventional text, students using Saxon's text and students using the other text showed no difference in achievement at the end of a year of algebra. This result must be compared to Saxon's (1986) paid advertisement, stating that, "The Saxon math books cause huge gains in comprehension, in test scores, and in math enrollment."

Whether or not Saxon's texts are better than conventional texts may depend to some extent on the ability of the students using his texts. The students in Johnson's study were above average, ranking as a class at the seventy-third percentile nationally. For such students, Saxon's texts may offer little advantage and may fail to challenge the more able students adequately. On the other hand, many of Saxon's supporters are primarily concerned with low-ability students and strongly believe these students are most apt to benefit from Saxon's approach.

Saxon clearly offers a different approach to teaching mathematics. Teachers and school districts impressed with Saxon's claims should consider carefully the significant differences in philosophy and approach between Saxon and the National Council of Teachers of Mathematics (see Chapter 3).

UCSMP: Redefining Middle School Mathematics

The University of Chicago School Mathematics Project began in 1983 with a six-year grant from the Amoco Foundation. Since that time, the Carnegie Corporation of New York, the National Science Foundation, the General Electric Foundation, GTE, Ford Motor Company, and Citicorp have also supported the project, which has developed into one of the largest university-based projects in mathematics education in the United States.

The aim of the UCSMP project is to develop and test a K–12 mathematics curriculum that will be meaningful for average students: that is, for students who will graduate from high school without taking advanced placement courses in mathematics. The seventh-grade text, *Transition Mathematics* (Usiskin et al. 1986) approaches this task by emphasizing the following concerns:

1. Wider scope, integrating arithmetic with introductory algebra and geometry.

2. Reading and problem solving. Every lesson requires reading and contains questions covering the reading.

3. Content and applications oriented to real-life experiences of students. Calculators are used extensively.

4. Four dimensions of understanding: skill in using algorithms; properties of mathematical relationships; concept development; and representation of ideas using pictures, manipulatives, and so forth.

5. An instructional format that consistently reviews concepts and practices skills until mastery is attained. Topics are arranged in chapters.

The UCSMP plan anticipates that about half of all eighth-graders would be ready for first-year algebra after using *Transition Mathematics* in the seventh grade. These students would then go on to geometry in the ninth grade and second-year algebra in the tenth grade. This would leave most students free to take advanced courses such as calculus, statistics, and computer science in the eleventh and twelfth grades. One consequence of this shift in the curriculum would be to expose American students to a variety and depth of mathematics comparable to that experienced by college-bound students in Japan and Europe. In field tests of *Transition Mathematics*, UCSMP project directors found that *"Transition Mathematics* students outperformed comparison students significantly in geometry and algebra readiness, and also became effective calculator users without a deterioration in their arithmetic skills" (UCSMP 1987). As with the Saxon publications, little independent evidence either supports or challenges these claims.

GEOMETRY: WHERE TOO MANY GIVE UP

Each year beyond grade nine, approximately half of all mathematics students take their last high school mathematics course and "drop out of the mathematics pipeline" (Steen 1989). For far too many high school students, tenth-grade geometry is the end of the line for their mathematics education. Only half of all high school students take geometry, and it is estimated that only 30 percent of these students master the course content at an A or B level of achievement. In most cases, the C, D, and F students in geometry do not go on to study algebra and trigonometry. The long-term effect of this decision is to make it impossible for 85 percent of our children to succeed in college programs emphasizing higher mathematics: engineering, economics, computer science, physics, chemistry, mathematics, and statistics.

The reason so many children fail to master geometry is now understood: A middle school curriculum that generally ignores the subject or fails to prepare students systematically for high school geometry. The nature of the problem is clearly illustrated when the current curriculum is contrasted with Van Hiele's widely accepted theory of what should take place in middle school geometry.

The Van Hiele Model

Pierre Van Hiele is now regarded as a major contributor to our understanding of how children learn geometry. Van Hiele's model of learning is similar to Piaget's in that it describes a sequence of categories or levels. However, Van Hiele's levels are levels of understanding of geometry, not levels of human development, although the two may be related. Many now believe that Van Hiele's model of understanding should become a model for guiding and informing the middle school mathematics curriculum.

The information in Table 2.1 summarizes the five levels of learning (0–4) in Van Hiele's model. To succeed in high school geometry, students should enter the class at Van Hiele level 2 or 3. In fact, most high school students enter geometry at level 0 or 1. No wonder so many fail! They are totally unprepared for the experience and attribute

Table 2.1   The Van Hiele Levels of Geometric Thought

Level	Learner Characteristics	Typical Task
0	The child experiences objects as a whole, unaware that they have specific attributes such as exactly four sides or an angle greater than 90°.	Name each object in a collection of squares, circles, and other shapes.
1	The child is now aware that objects have certain properties, although she or he still recognizes objects by the way they look instead of reflecting on their properties.	Given an object, list all of its properties: number of sides, number of angles, size of angles, etc.
2	At this level, the child realizes that the properties of an object, not the way it "looks," uniquely identify the object. Definitions and hierarchies make sense at this level.	Given a definition, draw the object. Create hierarchies of objects.
3	At this level, students reason from objects to relationships. Deductive logic makes sense.	Prove that two triangles can be congruent.
4	At this level, students can compare arguments and proofs.	Determine which of two proofs is better, and state why.

their failure to stupidity rather than lack of preparation. No wonder so many stop studying mathematics after they take geometry.

What Parents and Teachers Should Do

Middle school mathematics should devote a significant amount of time to working on geometry at levels 0, 1, and 2 of the Van Hiele model. Students should be tested to determine their Van Hiele level. As students master the tasks associated with each level, they should be given tasks that help them make the transition to the next level. Table 2.2 illustrates the type of tasks that students need to master at Van Hiele levels 0 through 2.

Teachers must recognize and accept that doing mathematics in this way will involve changes in their classroom routines. Parents must realize that such change is threatening to teachers, because the accepted routines direct and hold in check the considerable energies of a class of junior high school students. To teachers, a change in routine risks losing control; losing control risks losing their job and sanity. So parents ready to insist on meaningful change must also be prepared to support the teachers as they try out new teaching methodologies.

Parents may also take action at home by encouraging their children in mathematics every day. Bringing home library books that describe interesting careers in engineering and computer science would be a good start. Those who have a home computer should obtain a microcomputer software package. LOGO (available for most home computer systems) is now a part of many school computer-literacy programs. Elementary and junior high children will gladly spend hours playing in the geometrical world of LOGO, all the time learning and developing important insights at Van Hiele levels 0, 1, and 2. If your child is already taking high school geometry or will be during the next school year, the *Geometric Supposer* series of programs from Sunburst Publications is the best choice in software for children at Van Hiele level 2 and above.

Parents and teachers interested in a thorough discussion of Van Hiele's ideas should consider reading *The Van Hiele Model of Thinking in Geometry Among Adolescents* (Fuys, Geddes, and Tischler 1989) and *Structure and Insight: A Theory of Mathematics Education* (Van Hiele 1986).

Table 2.2 Van Hiele Level Descriptors and Sample Student Responses

Level 0: Student identifies and operates on shapes (e.g., squares, triangles) and other geometric configurations (e.g., lines, angles, grids) according to their appearance.

Level 0 Descriptors	Level 0 Sample Student Responses
The student	
1. identifies instances of a shape by its appearance as a whole	
a. in a simple drawing, diagram or set of cut-outs.	1a. Student identifies squares in a set of cut-out shapes or drawings.
b. in different positions.	1b. Student points out angles, rectangles, and triangles in different positions in a photograph or on a page of diagrams.
c. in a shape or other more complex configurations.	1c. Student points to the right angles in a trapezoid.
	Student outlines figures in a grid (e.g., angles, parallel lines, ladders).
2. constructs, draws, or copies a shape.	2. Student makes figures with D-stix; rectangle, parallel lines.
	Student makes a tiling pattern with cut-out triangles and copies the pattern (piece by piece) on paper.
3. names or labels shapes and other geometric configurations and uses standard and/or nonstandard names and labels appropriately.	3. Student points to angles of a triangle calling them "corners."

41

Level 0 Descriptors	Level 0 Sample Student Responses
	Student refers to angles by color (e.g., the "red angle") or by letter symbols (e.g., "angles A and B add to make C").
4. compares and sorts shapes on the basis of their appearance as a whole.	4. Student says "one is a square, the other is a rectangle" or "one is wider," when asked to say what is different about a cut-out square and rectangle.
	Student sorts cutout quads into "squares, rectangles, and others" because "they look alike."
5. verbally describes shapes by their appearance as a whole.	5. Student describes a rectangle as "looks like a square" or a parallelogram as "a slanty rectangle" or angle as "like hands on clock."
6. solves routine problems by operating on shapes rather than by using properties which apply in general.	6. Student uses trial-and-error approach to solve tangram puzzles such as making square and parallelogram pieces from two small triangle pieces.
	Student verifies that opposite sides of a rectangle are parallel by placing D-stix on edges.
	Student uses transparent "angle overlay" to find the measure of the third angle of a triangle.
	Student places square inch tiles on a rectangle and counts them to figure out the area of the rectangle.

7. identifies parts of a figure but

a. does **not** analyze a figure in terms of its components.

b. does **not** think of properties as characterizing a class of figures.

c. does **not** make generalizations about shapes or use related language.

7a. Student identifies squares by appearance as a whole, but does not spontaneously introduce "equal sides and right angles" or "square corners."

7b. Student points to sides of a square and measures to check they are equal but does not generalize equal sides for all squares.

7c. Student does not spontaneously use "all, some, every, none," and other such quantifiers in telling whether all, some, or none of a certain type of shape have a property.

Level 1: Student analyzes figures in terms of their components and relationships between components, establishes properties of a class of figures empirically, and uses properties to solve problems.

Level 1 Descriptors	Level 1 Sample Student Responses
The student	
1. identifies and tests relationships among components of figures (e.g., congruence of opposite sides of a parallelogram; congruence of angles in a tiling pattern).	1. Student points to sides and angles of a figure and spontaneously notes that "it has 4 right angles and all 4 sides are equal."

43

Level 1 Descriptors	Level 1 Sample Student Responses
2. recalls and uses appropriate vocabulary for components and relationships (e.g., opposite sides, corresponding angles are congruent, diagonals bisect each other).	2. Student observes that for a parallelogram "these opposite sides are parallel and so are these," checking with D-stix that the sides do not meet or are equally spaced.
3. a. compares two shapes according to relationships among their components.	3a. Student tells how a cut-out square and rectangle are alike and different in terms of their angles and sides.
b. sorts shapes in different ways according to certain properties, including a sort of all instances of a class from non-instances.	3b. Student makes up a rule for sorting quads—for example, according to number of right angles, or by number of pairs of parallel sides.
4. a. interprets and uses verbal description of a figure in terms of its properties and uses this description to draw/construct the figure.	4a. Student reads property cards "4 sides" and "all sides equal" and tries to draw a shape with these two properties that is not a square.
b. interprets verbal or symbolic statements of rules and applies them.	4b. When shown a property card for "saw," the student describes a saw and uses it to identify congruent angles in a grid.
	Student can explain the area rule—Area = length × width—for a rectangle and recognizes when it applies and does not apply.
5. discovers properties of specific figures empirically and generalizes properties for that class of figures.	5. After coloring in congruent angles in a triangular grid, student notes that "the three angles of the triangles are the same as the three angles that make a straight line and so the angle sum of the triangle is 180 degrees."

The student thinks this will work for other triangles and tries to verify this by using grids on other triangles.

After several instances of putting two congruent right triangles together to form a rectangle, the student says that you can find the area of a right triangle by making a rectangle and taking half its area.

From several numerical cases, the student discovers that the exterior angle of a triangle equals the sum of its two non-adjacent interior angles and believes that this is true for any triangle.

6a. Student describes a square over the telephone to a friend saying "it has 4 sides, 4 right angles, all sides are equal, and opposite sides are parallel."

6b. Given certain properties as clues about a shape, student tells what shape it must be on the basis of the properties.

7. Having noted that parallelograms have "opposite sides parallel," the student spontaneously adds "oh, so do these squares and these rectangles (pointing to these groups of sorted cutout quads).

6. a. describes a class of figures (e.g., parallelograms) in terms of its properties.

b. tells what shape a figure is, given certain properties.

7. identifies which properties used to characterize one class of figures also apply to another class of figures and compares classes of figures according to their properties.

Level 1 Descriptors	Level 1 Sample Student Responses
8. discovers properties of an unfamiliar class of figures.	8. After completing a sort of quads into kites and non-kites, the student discovers and verbalizes properties that characterize kites.
9. solves geometric problems by using known properties of figures or by insightful approaches.	9. When asked to find some angles in a photograph the student says "there are lots of angles because there are many triangles (pointing to them) and each has 3 angles."
	Student solves a problem about the line connecting the centers of two circles of equal radii and the line connecting the two points where the circles intersect. The student sees a rhombus in the diagram and observes that the lines are perpendicular because they are diagonals of the rhombus.
	Student figures out the angle sum of a quad is 360° because tiling yields the 4 angles around a point (i.e., 360°) or because the quad can be broken into two triangles ($180° + 180°$ = 360°).
	Student figures out how to find the area of a new shape by subdividing or transforming it into shapes whose areas he can already determine (e.g., a parallelogram into 2 triangles and a rectangle or into a rectangle).

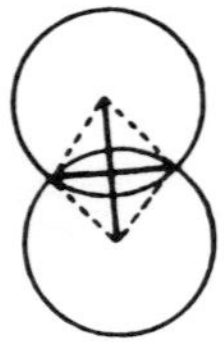

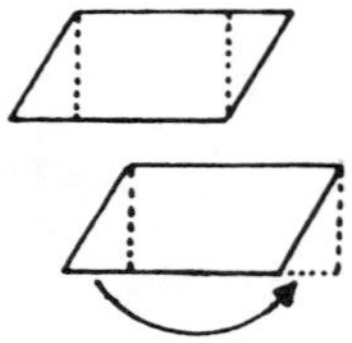

10. formulates and uses generalizations about properties of figures (guided by teacher/material or spontaneously on own) and uses related language (e.g., all, every, none) but

a. does **not** explain how certain properties of a figure are interrelated.

b. does **not** formulate and use formal definitions.

c. does **not** explain subclass relationships beyond checking specific instances against given list of properties.

d. does **not** see a need for proof or logical explanations of generalizations discovered empirically and does **not** use related language (e.g., if-then, because) correctly.

10a. When shown a parallelogram grid, the student cannot explain how the idea "opposite angles are equal" follows from "opposite sides are parallel."

10b. When asked to define a parallelogram, the student lists many properties but does not identify a set of necessary or a set of sufficient properties.

10c. After the student has listed the properties of all the members of the quad family, the student cannot explain why "all rectangles are parallelograms" or why "all squares are kites."

10d. After discovering the principle that the angle sum of a triangle is 180° by coloring angles in a triangle grid or by measuring, the student does not see any need for giving a deductive argument to show why the principle is valid.

Level 2 Descriptors	Level 2 Sample Student Responses
The student	
1. a. identifies different sets of properties that characterize a class of figures and tests that these are sufficient.	1a. Student selects properties that characterize a class of shapes (e.g., squares, parallelograms) and tests by drawings or construction with D-stix that these properties are sufficient.
	Student explains that two different sets of properties can be selected to characterize a class of parallelograms—either "4 sides" and "opposite sides are parallel" or "4 sides" and "opposite sides equal."
b. identifies minimum sets of properties that can characterize a figure.	1b. In describing a square to a friend, the student selects from a list of properties the fewest properties so the friend would be sure that the shape must be a "square."
c. formulates and uses a definition for a class of figures.	1c. Student formulates a definition of a kite and uses it to explain why figures are or are not kites.
2. gives informal arguments (using diagrams, cutout shapes that are folded, or other materials).	
a. having drawn a conclusion from given information, justifies the conclusion using logical relationships.	2a. Student concludes that "if angle A = angle B and angle C = angle B, then angle A = angle C because they both equal angle B."

When asked to explain why angle A = angle B in a triangle grid, the student says "the lines are parallel, and there is a saw (pointing to it), so angle A equals angle B by a saw."

b. orders classes of shapes.

2b. Student responds to the question "Is a rectangle a parallelogram?" by explaining "yes, because they have all the properties of a parallelogram, and also the special property of right angles."

Student uses the properties that characterize kites and squares to explain why all squares are kites but not all kites are squares.

c. orders two properties.

2c. Given a list of properties of a square, the student says "opposite sides are equal is not needed because it already says that all four sides are equal."

Having figured out a rule for the area of a right triangle from the rule for a rectangle, the student summarizes by making a family tree and explaining "you need this thought (rectangle rule) before this one (triangle rule)."

d. discovers new properties by deduction.

2d. Student explains that the two acute angles in any right triangle add up to 90° because "180 minus the right angle leaves 90, and that is what is left for the two acute angles."

Level 2 Descriptors	Level 2 Sample Student Responses
	Student deduces that the angle sum for any quad must be 360° "because the quad can be cut into two triangles, so 180° plus 180° makes 360°." When asked if it is possible to get $4 \times 180° = 720°$ for the angle sum if the quad were divided into 4 triangles (as shown here), the student explains that "No, the inside angles are not part of the quad's angles. So, if you do $4 \times 180°$, you have to take away the extra angles in the middle, and that gives $720° - 360°$ or $360°$ just as before." 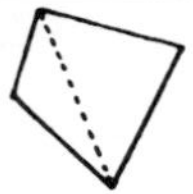 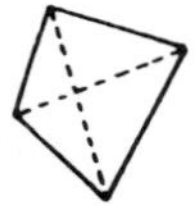
	Student discovers that the angle sum for a pentagon is 540° by breaking the pentagon into a quad (360°) and a triangle (180°) and says that this will work for any pentagon. 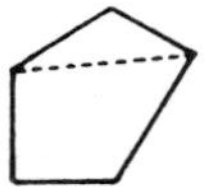
e. interrelates several properties in a family tree.	2e. Student arranges property cards to form a genealogical tree to show "ancestral" relationships—that is, student explains how "saws" and "straight angle = 180°" are ancestors of "angle sum of a triangle = 180°," and how this leads to "angle sum of a quad is 360°."
	Student tells how the area rule for a parallelogram can be derived from the area rule for a rectangle and puts this in a family tree.

3. gives informal deductive arguments.

a. follows a deductive argument and can supply parts of the argument.

b. gives a summary or variation of a deductive argument.

c. gives deductive arguments on own.

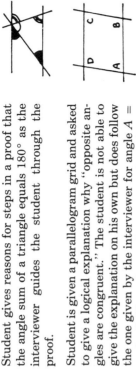

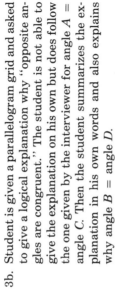

3a. Student gives reasons for steps in a proof that the angle sum of a triangle equals 180° as the interviewer guides the student through the proof.

3b. Student is given a parallelogram grid and asked to give a logical explanation why "opposite angles are congruent." The student is not able to give the explanation on his own but does follow the one given by the interviewer for angle A = angle C. Then the student summarizes the explanation in his own words and also explains why angle B = angle D.

Interviewer assists the student through a deductive explanation of why the exterior angle of a triangle (angle X) equals angle P + angle Q. Student summarizes this argument and then gives a complete argument on her own for a variation of this (i.e., angle Y = angle R + angle S).

3c. Student gives explanation on own for "opposite angles of a parallelogram are equal."

Student justifies why the area of a right triangle is ½ base × height, by explaining that two congruent right triangles make a rectangle. "If you put the two triangles together like this, you get opposite sides equal (since the triangles are

Level 2 Sample Student Responses

the same size). Angles B and D are right angles in the right triangles. Also, angles A and C are right angles because in a right triangle the two smaller angles together make 90°. Angle Z is the same as angle X so angles Y and Z add up to 90°. So the shape must be a rectangle, and the right triangle must be half the area of the rectangle."

4. Student gives two different explanations why the angle sum of a triangle equals 180°—either by two saws or by a saw and a ladder. The two ways are then shown by two different family trees.

Student explains the angle sum of a pentagon equals 540° by dividing it into three triangles ($3 \times 180°$) or by dividing it into a quad and a triangle ($360° + 180°$) and showing each method by a family tree.

5. In a discussion of saws and ladders, the student discovers that "Oh, if the angles are made equal, then the lines are parallel" and "Oh, now if the lines are parallel, then the angles are equal." When asked if these are the same statements, the student realizes "No, in one you start with parallel lines and make the angles equal, and in the other you do the opposite."

Level 2 Descriptors

4. gives more than one explanation to prove something and justifies these explanations by using family trees.

5. informally recognizes difference between a statement and its converse.

52

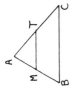

6. Given the problem that M is the midpoint of AB in triangle ABC, and MT is parallel to BC, find the ratio of MT to BC, the student uses the strategy of ladder to get congruent angles and hence similar triangles. So since $AM:AB$ as 1:2, then $MT \cdot BC$ as 1:2.

Given two intersecting circles A and B, not with the same radii, and a common chord CD, show that AB is perpendicular to CD. The student proves this by establishing that $ADBC$ must be a kite and then the perpendicularity of its diagnosis makes AB perpendicular to CD.

7. Student recognizes the role of logical explanations or deductive arguments in establishing facts (versus an inductive, empirical approach) and says (after giving a logical explanation) "I know that the angle sum for every pentagon is 540° and I don't have to measure." However, the student has yet to experience "proof" in an axiomatic sense (i.e., using postulates, axioms, definitions) and so is uncertain when asked about possible "ancestors" to the saw and ladder principles.

6. identifies and uses strategies or insightful reasoning to solve problems.

7. recognizes the role of deductive argument and approaches problems in a deductive manner but

a. does **not** grasp the meaning of deduction in an axiomatic sense (e.g., does **not** see the need for definitions and basic assumptions).

b. does **not** formally distinguish between a statement and its converse (e.g., cannot separate the "Siamese twins"—the statement and its converse).

c. does **not** yet establish interrelationships between networks of theorems.

Reproduced with permission from *The Van Hiele Model of Thinking in Geometry among Adolescents*, copyright 1988 by the National Council of Teachers of Mathematics.

SUMMARY

During grades five through eight, children begin to develop the capacity for abstract thought. Piaget called this level of thought "formal operations." This new capacity manifests itself in questioning behavior that rejects authority as a justification in its own right. To such people, instruction must be both logical and relevant if it is to be valued.

The National Council of Teachers of Mathematics (NCTM) has prepared recommendations for the middle school mathematics curriculum that emphasize problem solving and meaningful skills. These recommendations include an emphasis on proper preparation for high school geometry, based on a theory of learning developed by Pierre Van Hiele. Local school districts should review their current programs for grades five through eight, to determine whether those programs are in harmony with the NCTM guidelines.

DISCUSSION QUESTIONS

1. If children all switched to formal operational thought at age twelve and no longer needed concrete manipulatives, junior high school might start to look more like college than elementary school. Instead, the transition is gradual and often overlooked in the general chaos of puberty and adolescence. What changes in behavior might a teacher look for that reveal a new kind of readiness for mathematics?

2. Support or challenge the following statement:

   Middle school and junior high mathematics students should be required to master arithmetic before attempting pre-algebra or pre-geometry.

3. Support or challenge the following statement:

   Middle school and junior high mathematics students should not be allowed to use calculators for homework, quizzes, or exams.

4. Examine copies of Saxon's junior high mathematics texts. How do you feel about the content? About Saxon's approach? Do you consider the texts complete as a course or would you want to supplement the content with other materials and activities?

5. Examine a copy of a more conventional junior high mathematics text. How do you feel about the content? About the approach? Do you consider the text complete as a course, or would you want to supplement the content with other materials and activities?

6. Using the Van Hiele levels outlined in Table 2.1 and the items found in Table 2.2 as a guide, interview several students in grades five through nine. At what Van Hiele levels would you place them? Where would you place yourself? Now take a high school geometry book and look at the first three chapters. What Van Hiele level is assumed?

REFERENCES AND SUGGESTED READINGS

Burger, William F. "Geometry."*Arithmetic Teacher,* vol. 32, no. 6 (Feb. 1985), 52–56.

Curriculum and Evaluation Standards for School Mathematics. Reston, VA: National Council of Teachers of Mathematics, 1989.

Fuys, David, Dorothy Geddes, and Rosamond Tischler. *The Van Hiele Model of Thinking in Geometry among Adolescents.* Reston, VA: National Council of Teachers of Mathematics, 1989.

Geometry for Grades K-6. Readings from the Arithmetic Teacher, edited by Jane M. Hill. Reston, VA: National Council of Teachers of Mathematics, 1987.

Hoffer, Alan. "Geometry Is More Than Proof." *Mathematics Teacher,* vol. 74, no. 1 (Jan. 1981), 11–18.

Johnson, Dale M. "An Evaluation of Saxon's Algebra Text." *Journal of Educational Research,* vol. 81, no. 2 (Nov.–Dec. 1987), 97–102.

Saxon, John. *Algebra 1: An Incremental Development.* Norman, OK: Saxon Publishers, 1981.

Saxon, John. *Math 76: An Incremental Development.* Norman, OK: Saxon Publishers, 1985.

Saxon, John. [Paid advertisement]. *Mathematics Teacher,* vol. 79, no. 1 (1986), 22.

Saxon, John. *Math 65: An Incremental Development.* Norman, OK: Saxon Publishers, 1987.

Shaughnessy, Michael, and William F. Burger. "Spadework Prior to Deduction in Geometry." *Mathematics Teacher,* vol. 78, no. 6 (Sept. 1985), 419–428.

Steen, Lynn A. "Insularity in the Mathematical Sciences Has Seriously Weakened Mathematics Education." *Chronicle of Higher Education,* vol. 35, no. 28 (March 22,1989), B2–B3.

Usiskin, Zalman. "The UCSMP: Translating Grades 7–12 Mathematics into Reality." *Educational Leadership,* vol. 44, no. 4 (Dec. 1986–Jan. 1987), 30–35.

Usiskin, Zalman, et al. *Transition Mathematics.* Chicago: University of Chicago School Mathematics Project, 1986.

Van Hiele, Pierre M. *Structure and Insight: A Theory of Mathematics Education.* Orlando, FL: Academic Press, 1986.

CHAPTER 3

How Are We Doing and Where Are We Going?

In 1983, the United States Secretary of Education, speaking on behalf of the National Commission on Excellence in Education, startled the American public with the following statement:

> Our nation is at risk. Our once unchallenged preeminence in commerce, industry, science, and technological innovation is being overtaken by competitors throughout the world. . . . The educational foundations of our society are presently being eroded by a rising tide of mediocrity that threatens our very future as a Nation and a people. (National Commission 1983)

With this assertion, the U.S. Secretary of Education ushered in a period of critical self-analysis in American education. Since *A Nation at Risk* appeared, a number of other national commissions and profes-

57

sional organizations have contributed to our understanding of what is wrong and right with American mathematics education. Significant findings of several such reports are presented here.

THE SECOND INTERNATIONAL MATHEMATICS STUDY

Near the end of the 1981–1982 school year, 12,000 students from 500 mathematics classrooms in about 250 public and private schools were randomly selected to represent the United States in the Second International Mathematics Study (SIMS). The purpose of the SIMS study was to investigate the teaching and learning of mathematics in the schools of twenty countries around the world.

Since it is not practical to examine all aspects of the mathematics education programs of each of twenty countries, SIMS singled out two groups of students for investigation: eighth-graders, and high school seniors enrolled in advanced, college preparatory mathematics courses.

Among the many findings of the SIMS study, the following are indicative of the achievement of eighth graders as measured by a standardized mathematics examination (McKnight 1987a):

- Japan obtained the highest scores.
- The United States performed at about the international average in the areas of computational arithmetic and algebra.
- The United States performed well below the international average in problem-solving and geometry.

Findings regarding twelfth graders included the following:

- Hong Kong and Japan were the top performers.
- The best calculus students in the United States were near the average for the rest of the world.
- The performance of the United States in pre-calculus was well below the international average.

These findings suggest that America's problems with mathematics begin in elementary school and only get worse in high school. A natural question in light of this observation is, "How is American education different from that of other countries?" To address this question, the SIMS study investigated a number of factors related to teaching and learning. The findings of this aspect of the study include the following observations:

- Homework levels in the United States were slightly above the international average.

- American students are exposed to a narrower range of topics and study topics in less depth than the international average.

- Class sizes in the United States are near the international average.

- Total number of hours of mathematics instruction for our students was at about the international average at the eighth-grade level.

- At the twelfth-grade level, our students spent less time than the international average in studying mathematics.

- American teachers appear to have about the same mathematical background as their counterparts in other countries.

- American teachers of mathematics have teaching loads greater than those of their Japanese counterparts.

These findings led the team of American SIMS researchers and educators to make the following recommendations, among others, for change in American mathematics education:

- Eliminate excessive repetition of topics.

- Go deeper into a variety of topics.

- Introduce geometry, probability, and statistics to the junior high curriculum.

- Increase the rewards and expectations of educators, emphasizing professional growth.

Significantly, three of these recommendations suggest that flaws in the American mathematics curriculum are strongly related to the low academic achievement of American mathematics students. If carried out, these recommendations for change would reshape American mathematics education. However, to many adults, questioning the wisdom of the mathematics curriculum that shaped their own lives may seem reckless. Nevertheless, persons attempting to prepare the next generation of citizens for adult life in the twenty-first century have serious doubts that the current curriculum is still a valid preparation.

> Every weekday, 25 million children study mathematics in our nation's schools. Those at the younger end, some 15 million of them, will enter the adult world in the period 1995–2000. The 40 classroom minutes they spend on mathematics each day are largely devoted to mastery of skills which would have been needed by a shopkeeper in the year 1940—skills needed by virtually no one today. Almost no time is spent on estimation, probability, interest, histograms, spreadsheets, or real problem-solving—things which will be common-place in most of these people's lives. While the 15 million of them sit there drilling away on those arithmetic or algebraic exercises, their future options are bit-by-bit eroded. (McKnight 1987b)

EDUCATING AMERICANS FOR THE TWENTY-FIRST CENTURY

Calls for change in the mathematics curriculum have not been limited to secondary-level mathematics. In 1983, The National Science Board Commission on Precollege Education in Mathematics, Science, and Technology made the following recommendations for elementary and middle school mathematics (National Science Board 1983):

- Calculators and computers should be used as early as possible to enhance the understanding of arithmetic and geometry and the learning of problem-solving.

Table 3.1   Access to Calculators for Use in Mathematics Class, Grades 3, 7, and 11: 1986*

	Percent "Yes"		
	Grade 3	Grade 7	Grade 11
Do you or your family own a calculator?	82 (0.9)	94 (0.7)	97 (0.7)
Does your school have calculators for use in math class?	15 (1.1)	21 (1.6)	26 (1.9)

*Jackknifed standard errors are presented in parentheses.
Reproduced with permission from John Dossey et al.; *The Mathematics Report Card: Are We Measuring Up?*, Educational Testing Service, 1988.

- Substantially more emphasis should be placed on the development of skills in mental arithmetic, estimation, and approximation, and less emphasis given to paper-and-pencil exercises in arithmetic operations.

However, as of 1986, *The Mathematics Report Card: Are We Measuring Up?* (Dossey et al. 1988) reported that "most students have calculators available in the home, but relatively few have access to calculators in school (see Table 3.1).

Learning when and how to estimate by using mental arithmetic is as essential a task in the development of "number sense" as the ability to use calculators and computers in computation and problem-solving. Unfortunately, few teachers incorporate mental arithmetic and estimation into routine mathematics instruction.

THE MATHEMATICS REPORT CARD

Based on the 1986 National Assessment of Educational Progress, *The Mathematics Report Card: Are We Measuring Up?* (Dossey et al. 1988) offers an overview of the mathematics achievement of the nation's nine-, thirteen-, and seventeen-year-old students. In the report, five levels of proficiency in mathematics are defined:

Level 150   Simple arithmetic facts
Level 200   Beginning skills and understanding
Level 250   Basic operations and beginning problem solving
Level 300   Moderately complex procedures and reasoning
Level 350   Multi-step problem solving and algebra

Using these levels as references, Table 3.2 shows the average mathematics proficiency of over 100,000 nine- and thirteen-year-olds as measured by the National Assessment of Educational Progress (NAEP) in 1977–1978, 1981–1982, and 1985–1986. For both nine- and thirteen-year-olds, the table shows a slight overall improvement over the period 1977–1986 for both ages and both sexes.

Table 3.3 provides a more detailed analysis of the nine-year-olds with respect to levels 150–300. Table 3.4 looks at the performance of thirteen-year-olds at levels 200–350.

Although those tables indicate no decline in overall mathematical proficiency during the years 1977–1986, a number of concerns emerge from an analysis of the data.

- Over one-fourth of nine-year-olds do not perform at the 200 level. This translates into approximately 700,000 nine-year-olds nationwide who do not possess basic mathematical skills and concepts.

- Approximately one-fourth of thirteen-year-olds (roughly 750,000 eighth-graders nationwide) do not possess the skills in whole number operations needed to perform many everyday tasks.

- Less than one-sixth of thirteen-year-olds are proficient at the 300 level. This represents a decline over the period 1977–1986 and indicates a mathematics curriculum which is severely limited in terms of its variety and attention to problem solving.

In general, it seems that the modest progress made during the period 1977–1986 primarily represents better performance on low-level skills. Indeed, achievement with respect to higher-level skills has slipped over the same period. So one might say that the students got better at routine computational tasks while slipping farther behind on problem solving. Another way to look at the situation is to say that between grades three and seven, school mathematics appears to em-

Table 3.2 Mean Mathematics Proficiency

Weighted mathematics proficiency means and jackknifed standard errors

	1977–78	1981–82	1985–86
Age 9			
Total	218.6(0.8)	219.0(1.1)	221.7(1.0)
Sex			
Male	217.4(0.7)	217.1(1.2)	221.7(1.1)
Female	219.9(1.0)	220.8(1.2)	221.7(1.2)
Ethnicity/race			
White	224.1(0.9)	224.0(1.1)	226.9(1.1)
Black	192.4(1.1)	194.9(1.6)	201.6(1.6)
Hispanic	202.9(2.3)	204.0(1.3)	205.4(2.1)
Region			
Northeast	226.9(1.9)	225.7(1.7)	226.0(2.7)
Southeast	208.9(1.2)	210.4(2.9)	217.8(2.5)
Central	224.0(1.5)	221.1(2.4)	226.0(2.3)
West	213.5(1.4)	219.3(1.7)	217.2(2.4)
Parental education			
Less than H.S.	200.3(1.5)	199.0(1.7)	200.6(2.5)
Graduated H.S.	219.2(1.1)	218.3(1.1)	218.4(1.6)
Some educ after H.S.	230.1(1.7)	225.2(2.1)	228.6(2.1)
Graduated college	231.3(1.1)	228.8(1.5)	231.3(1.1)
Age 13			
Total	264.1(1.1)	266.6(1.1)	269.0(1.2)
Sex			
Male	263.6(1.3)	269.2(1.4)	270.0(1.1)
Female	264.7(1.1)	268.0(1.1)	268.0(1.5)
Ethnicity/race			
White	271.6(0.9)	274.4(1.0)	273.6(1.3)
Black	229.6(1.9)	240.4(1.6)	249.2(2.3)
Hispanic	238.0(2.2)	252.4(1.6)	254.3(2.9)
Region			
Northeast	272.7(2.4)	276.9(2.2)	276.6(2.2)
Southeast	252.7(3.2)	258.1(2.4)	263.5(1.4)
Central	269.4(1.8)	272.8(1.9)	266.1(4.5)
West	260.0(1.9)	266.0(2.3)	270.4(2.1)
Parental education			
Less than H.S.	244.7(1.2)	251.0(1.4)	252.3(2.3)
Graduated H.S.	263.1(1.0)	262.9(0.8)	262.7(1.2)
Some educ after H.S.	273.1(1.2)	275.1(0.9)	273.7(0.8)
Graduated college	283.8(1.3)	282.3(1.5)	279.9(1.4)

Reproduced with permission from John Dossey et al., *The Mathematics Report Card: Are We Measuring Up?* (Educational Testing Service, 1988).

Table 3.3 Percentage of Students Age 9 at or Above the Five Mathematics Proficiency Levels

Simple Arithmetic Facts (150)

Weighted percentage of 9-year-old students with mathematics proficiency at or above 150

	1977–78	1981–82	1985–86
Total	96.5(0.2)	97.2(0.3)	97.8(0.2)
Sex			
Male	95.9(0.3)	96.8(0.4)	97.7(0.3)
Female	97.2(0.3)	97.6(0.3)	98.0(0.3)
Ethnicity/race			
White	98.3(0.2)	98.6(0.2)	98.9(0.2)
Black	87.8(0.9)	90.4(1.0)	93.0(1.2)
Hispanic	93.5(1.1)	95.0(1.0)	96.4(1.0)
Region			
Northeast	97.8(0.4)	98.4(0.4)	98.6(0.4)
Southeast	94.0(0.6)	94.7(0.9)	96.9(0.7)
Central	98.0(0.3)	98.0(0.4)	98.9(0.3)
West	96.1(0.5)	97.7(0.5)	97.0(0.8)
Parental education			
Less than H.S.	91.2(0.8)	91.6(1.2)	94.7(1.7)
Graduated H.S.	96.9(0.3)	97.7(0.3)	97.7(0.4)
Some educ after H.S.	98.6(0.4)	98.5(0.5)	98.0(0.8)
Graduated college	98.6(0.2)	98.5(0.3)	99.1(0.2)

Beginning Skills and Understanding (200)

Weighted percentage of 9-year-old students with mathematics proficiency at or above 200

	1977–78	1981–82	1985–86
Total	70.3(0.9)	71.5(1.1)	73.9(1.1)
Sex			
Male	68.7(0.9)	68.8(1.2)	74.0(1.1)
Female	71.9(1.0)	74.2(1.2)	73.9(1.3)
Ethnicity/race			
White	76.0(0.9)	76.9(1.1)	79.2(1.2)
Black	42.5(1.3)	46.7(2.3)	53.3(2.4)
Hispanic	54.3(2.6)	55.0(1.9)	58.7(2.5)

Weighted percentage of 9-year-old students with mathematics proficiency at or above 200

	1977–78	1981–82	1985–86
Region			
Northeast	78.4(2.1)	78.1(1.9)	78.8(2.9)
Southeast	60.7(1.7)	62.7(2.6)	69.9(2.5)
Central	75.1(1.5)	74.1(2.3)	76.5(2.3)
West	65.9(1.6)	71.7(2.1)	70.9(2.9)
Parental education			
Less than H.S.	51.2(1.9)	52.4(1.8)	49.4(3.4)
Graduated H.S.	72.1(1.3)	72.4(1.1)	72.5(1.9)
Some educ after H.S.	79.9(1.2)	76.6(2.1)	79.7(1.8)
Graduated college	82.3(1.2)	79.5(1.4)	82.5(1.1)

Basic Operations and Beginning Problem Solving (250)

Weighted pecentage of 9-year-old students with mathematics proficiency at or above 250

	1977–78	1981–82	1985–86
Total	19.4(0.6)	18.7(0.8)	20.8(0.9)
Sex			
Male	18.9(0.5)	18.2(0.9)	20.6(0.9)
Female	19.8(0.7)	19.2(0.9)	20.9(1.1)
Ethnicity/race			
White	22.5(0.7)	21.5(0.9)	24.5(1.0)
Black	4.3(0.5)	4.5(0.5)	5.4(0.7)
Hispanic	10.8(1.3)	9.2(1.1)	8.0(2.5)
Region			
Northeast	24.9(1.0)	23.6(1.3)	25.0(2.6)
Southeast	13.1(0.7)	13.5(1.6)	17.1(2.2)
Central	23.0(1.2)	19.2(2.0)	24.8(1.7)
West	15.6(1.0)	19.0(1.2)	16.2(2.0)
Parental education			
Less than H.S.	7.8(0.8)	7.6(0.7)	6.2(2.0)
Graduated H.S.	19.2(1.0)	16.2(0.9)	17.4(1.4)
Some educ after H.S.	29.0(1.4)	24.3(2.7)	26.4(2.0)
Graduated college	30.9(1.1)	27.1(1.2)	29.4(1.2)

Moderately Complex Procedures and Reasoning (300)

Weighted percentage of 9-year-old students with mathematics proficiency at or above 300

	1977–78	1981–82	1985–86
Total	0.8(0.1)	0.6(0.1)	0.6(0.2)
Sex			
Male	0.7(0.1)	0.6(0.1)	0.6(0.3)
Female	0.8(0.2)	0.6(0.1)	0.5(0.2)
Ethnicity/race			
White	0.9(0.1)	0.7(0.1)	0.7(0.2)
Black	0.0(0.0)	0.0(0.0)	0.0(0.0)
Hispanic	0.5(0.4)	0.0(0.0)	0.0(0.0)
Region			
Northeast	1.1(0.3)	1.2(0.2)	0.8(0.3)
Southeast	0.3(0.1)	0.3(0.1)	0.2(0.1)
Central	1.3(0.2)	0.5(0.2)	0.9(0.6)
West	0.2(0.1)	0.5(0.1)	0.3(0.1)
Parental education			
Less than H.S.	0.2(0.1)	0.0(0.0)	0.0(0.0)
Graduated H.S.	0.8(0.1)	0.2(0.1)	0.1(0.1)
Some educ after H.S.	1.8(0.5)	0.9(0.4)	0.8(0.5)
Graduated college	1.3(0.2)	1.2(0.2)	1.1(0.4)

(Virtually no 9-year-old students had mathematics proficiency at level 350.)
Reproduced with permission from John Dossey et al., *The Mathematics Report Card: Are We Measuring Up?* (Edcuational Testing Service, 1988).

phasize basic computational skills while deemphasizing problem solving and mathematical applications. Given this trend away from applications, it is not surprising to learn that over the period 1977–1986, a decreasing percentage of thirteen-year-olds indicated that they would like to take more mathematics.

This lack of interest in mathematics shows up in decreasing enrollments in high school mathematics. For instance, approximately half of all students take their last high school mathematics course in the ninth grade. Of the students who take mathematics in the tenth grade, only about half go on to take mathematics as juniors. Perhaps half of those students go on to take mathematics as seniors. Thus, only

Table 3.4 Percentage of Students Age 13 at or Above the Five Mathematics Proficiency Levels

(Virtually all 13-year-old students had mathematics proficiency at or above level 150)

Beginning Skills and Understanding (200)

Weighted percentage of 13-year-old students with mathematics proficiency at or above 200

	1977–78	1981–82	1985–86
Total	94.5(0.4)	97.6(0.4)	98.5(0.2)
Sex			
Male	93.8(0.5)	97.3(0.5)	98.3(0.3)
Female	95.1(0.4)	97.9(0.2)	98.7(0.3)
Ethnicity/race			
White	97.5(0.2)	99.1(0.1)	99.2(0.3)
Black	79.5(1.4)	89.0(1.3)	95.5(0.8)
Hispanic	85.9(0.9)	96.1(0.8)	96.1(1.1)
Region			
Northeast	96.1(0.7)	98.8(0.3)	99.3(0.2)
Southeast	90.3(1.5)	95.3(1.0)	98.6(0.3)
Central	96.9(0.4)	98.5(0.4)	98.0(1.0)
West	93.6(0.8)	97.5(0.9)	98.2(0.4)
Parental education			
Less than H.S.	88.9(0.9)	95.2(1.2)	96.9(0.8)
Graduated H.S.	95.9(0.4)	97.8(0.4)	98.5(0.3)
Some educ after H .S.	97.8(0.4)	98.7(0.2)	99.5(0.3)
Graduated college	98.8(0.2)	98.7(0.4)	99.1(0.2)

Basic Operations and Beginning Problem Solving (250)

Weighted percentage of 13-year-old students with mathematics proficiency at or above 250

	1977–78	1981–82	1985–86
Total	64.9(1.2)	71.6(1.2)	73.1(1.5)
Sex			
Male	63.7(1.3)	70.9(1.4)	74.0(1.7)
Female	66.1(1.2)	72.3(1.1)	72.3(1.8)

Weighted percentage of 13-year-old students with mathematics proficiency at or above 250

	1977–78	1981–82	1985–86
Ethnicity/race			
White	72.9(0.8)	78.5(0.9)	78.7(1.6)
Black	28.9(1.8)	38.1(1.7)	49.4(3.6)
Hispanic	35.6(2.5)	54.2(2.1)	55.2(4.9)
Region			
Northeast	73.6(2.3)	79.6(1.6)	80.4(2.2)
Southeast	54.2(3.4)	60.5(2.1)	68.1(1.9)
Central	70.0(1.8)	76.2(2.0)	71.2(6.1)
West	60.0(2.2)	69.2(2.9)	73.5(2.1)
Parental education			
Less than H.S.	43.6(1.5)	50.1(1.6)	56.3(3.5)
Graduated H.S.	64.6(1.1)	67.4(0.9)	68.9(1.4)
Some educ after H.S.	75.6(1.4)	80.6(1.2)	80.3(1.6)
Graduated college	84.2(1.1)	84.5(1.4)	83.0(1.4)

Moderately Complex Procedures and Reasoning (300)

Weighted percentage of 13-year-old students with mathematics proficiency at or above 300

	1977–78	1981–82	1985–86
Total	17.9(0.7)	17.8(0.9)	15.9(1.0)
Sex			
Male	18.3(0.8)	19.2(1.1)	17.6(1.0)
Female	17.4(0.7)	16.3(0.9)	14.2(1.3)
Ethnicity/race			
White	21.4(0.7)	20.9(0.9)	18.6(1.1)
Black	2.1(0.4)	3.3(0.9)	4.0(1.4)
Hispanic	3.4(0.6)	6.2(1.0)	5.4(1.0)
Region			
Northeast	24.3(1.8)	24.3(2.3)	22.0(2.4)
Southeast	11.6(1.4)	10.3(1.4)	10.8(1.1)
Central	20.8(1.3)	20.3(1.4)	12.6(2.4)
West	13.8(1.0)	15.6(1.6)	18.4(2.2)
Parental education			
Less than H.S.	5.8(0.6)	5.4(0.7)	5.3(1.2)
Graduated H.S.	15.0(0.7)	10.6(0.6)	7.8(0.8)
Some educ after H.S.	22.5(0.8)	20.5(1.2)	17.7(1.4)
Graduated college	32.0(1.4)	31.3(1.3)	25.6(1.3)

Multi-Step Problem Solving and Algebra (350)

Weighted percentage of 13-year-old students with mathematics proficiency at or above 350

	1977–78	1981–82	1985–86
Total	0.9(0.2)	0.5(0.1)	0.4(0.1)
Sex			
Male	1.0(0.2)	0.7(0.1)	0.6(0.2)
Female	0.8(0.2)	0.3(0.1)	0.2(0.1)
Ethnicity/race			
White	1.1(0.2)	0.6(0.1)	0.5(0.1)
Black	0.0(0.0)	0.0(0.0)	0.1(0.1)
Hispanic	0.1(0.1)	0.2(0.1)	0.3(0.4)
Region			
Northeast	1.4(0.6)	1.2(0.5)	0.7(0.3)
Southeast	0.5(0.1)	0.2(0.1)	0.2(0.1)
Central	1.1(0.2)	0.5(0.1)	0.2(0.2)
West	0.7(0.2)	0.3(0.1)	0.6(0.3)
Parental education			
Less than H.S.	0.1(0.1)	0.0(0.0)	0.0(0.0)
Graduated H.S.	0.3(0.1)	0.1(0.0)	0.2(0.1)
Some educ after H.S.	0.7(0.1)	0.4(0.1)	0.5(0.3)
Graduated college	2.7(0.6)	1.4(0.4)	0.6(0.2)

Reproduced with permission from John Dossey et al., *The Mathematics Report Card: Are We Measuring Up?* (Educational Testing Service, 1988).

a small percentage of students complete high school with four years of mathematics. Individually and as a nation, this costs us in terms of lost opportunity. Left unchecked, the trend may well cost us our standard of living, as international competitors outperform us professionally and economically.

EVERYBODY COUNTS

Mathematics education is facing a number of serious problems in the United States. In *Everybody Counts: A Report to the Nation on the*

Future of Mathematics Education (National Research Council 1989), the following challenges, among others, are identified:

- Far too many students leave school without having acquired the mathematial power necessary for productive lives.

- On average, U.S. students do not master mathematical fundamentals at a level sufficient to sustain our present technologically based society.

- When compared with other nations, U.S. students lag far behind in level of mathematical accomplishment; the resulting educational deficit reduces our ability to compete in international arenas.

- Curricula and instruction in our schools and colleges are years behind the times. They reflect neither the increased demand for higher-order thinking skills, nor the greatly expanded uses of the mathematical sciences, nor what we know about the best ways for students to learn mathematics.

- Calculators and computers have had virtually no impact on mathematics instruction, in spite of their great potential to enrich, enlighten, and expand students' learning of mathematics.

In order to respond effectively to these and other challenges, the National Research Council's Board on Mathematical Sciences in *Everybody Counts,* recommends the following changes in American mathematics education:

- Shift the focus of school mathematics, from its current dualistic approach (minimal mathematics for the majority of students; advanced mathematics for a few students) to a common core of mathematics for all students throughout their school experience.

- Shift the focus from the teacher to the student by emphasizing simulation, participation, and exploration of ideas.

- Educate the public about the importance of mathematics in our technological society.

- Spend more time on developing broad-based mathematical problem-solving skills and less time on perfecting routine arithmetic computation.

- Emphasize the relevance of mathematics to students' present and future needs.

- Teach students to use calculators and computers effectively. Deemphasize paper-and-pencil computation.

- Emphasize the perception of mathematics as an active pattern-finding tool. Deemphasize the traditional perception of mathematics as a fixed body of rules.

Leadership

Effecting these changes will take a great deal of talent and effort. The following recommendations for action (National Research Council 1989) make it clear that there is a role for every concerned student, teacher, administrator, and citizen in this task. These recommendations are reproduced with permission from *Everybody Counts: A Report to the Nation on the Future of Mathematics Education*, copyright 1989 by the National Academy of Sciences.

Students

- Study mathematics every school year.
- Discover the mathematics that is all around us.
- Use mathematics in other classes and in daily life.
- Study a broad variety of mathematical subjects.

Teachers

- Talk with each other about mathematics.
- Examine current practice and debate new proposals.
- Engage students actively in the process of learning.

Parents

- Demand that schools meet the new NCTM Standards.
- Encourage children to continue studying mathematics.

- Support teachers who seek curricular improvements.
- Expect homework to be more than routine computation.

Principals

- Provide opportunities for teachers to work together.
- Become educated on issues in mathematics education.
- Support innovation.
- Encourage paired teaching in elementary school.

Superintendents

- Stimulate public discussion of mathematics education.
- Provide resources for curricular innovation.
- Support a climate of change.

School Boards

- Establish approximate standards for mathematics.
- Align assessment with curricular goals.
- Support innovation and professional development.

Community Organizations

- Enrich mathematical opportunities for all students.
- Support local efforts to improve mathematics education.
- Explain to the public the need for a change.

State School Officers

- Promote adoption of NCTM standards.
- Encourage use of elementary mathematics specialists.
- Speak out publicly about mathematics education.
- Stress assessment of high-order thinking.

College and University Faculty

- Make introductory courses attractive and effective.
- Restore integrity to the undergraduate program.
- Lecture less; try other teaching methods.
- Link scholarship to teaching.

College and University Administrators

- Reward curricular innovation and good teaching.
- Recognize that mathematics classes need computer labs.
- Diminish reliance on underpaid, part-time faculty.
- Emphasize and improve teacher education.

Business and Industry

- Encourage students to study mathematics and science.
- Do not steal good teachers by hiring them away.
- Support local efforts to secure funds for education.
- Support strong continuing education, not remediation.
- Provide internship opportunities for teachers.

State Legislators

- Work with school leaders to support effective programs.
- Recognize that mathematics education is an investment.
- Resist pressures for simplistic cures.

Governors

- Provide resources to encourage change.
- Demand new standards for mathematics education.
- Lead the public to make wise choices among priorities.
- Create enrichment programs for able students.

Congress

- Stress education as an essential investment.
- Support mathematics education at all levels.
- Reward effective programs.

The President

- Meet with state governors to affirm the national agenda.
- Focus public attention on mathematics education.
- Stress education as crucial to national security.

THE NCTM CURRICULUM AND EVALUATION STANDARDS

The National Council of Teachers of Mathematics' *Curriculum and Evaluation Standards for School Mathematics* (NCTM 1989) provides a clear picture of what the K–12 mathematics curriculum ought to emphasize. If parents, teachers, administrators, and governmental leaders want to know what the leadership of American mathematics education wants, that publication is the place to start reading.

Goals for K–4 Mathematics

Several assumptions shaped the development of the NCTM curriculum standards for K–4 mathematics. These assumptions state that the K–4 curriculum should

1. Be conceptually oriented;

2. Actively involve children in doing mathematics;

3. Emphasize the development of mathematical thinking and reasoning abilities;

4. Emphasize the application of mathematics;

5. Include a wide variety of content;

6. Make appropriate use of calculators and computers.

The goals of the K–4 curriculum are to help students learn the value of mathematics, become confident of their ability to do mathematics, become mathematical problem-solvers, communicate mathematically, and reason mathematically.

Thirteen curriculum standards for grades K–4 define the content of the curriculum.

1. *Mathematics as problem solving:* By learning to represent real-life problems by using mathematical ideas and language, and by learning problem-solving strategies that work in a wide variety of problem situations, students gain confidence in their ability to do

mathematics and an appreciation for mathematics as a practical life tool.

> *Example:* I have six coins worth 75 cents. What coins do you think I have? Is there more than one answer?

2. *Mathematics as communication:* Students need to develop a variety of specialized reading, writing, speaking, and listening skills appropriate to mathematics classrooms. The use of manipulatives, pictures, and diagrams is also an important part of conceptualizing and communicating mathematics.

> *Example:* Make up and solve a problem about sharing a candy bar with three of your friends.

3. *Mathematics as reasoning:* Whenever a student makes an assertion about some mathematical idea, the bases of the assertion should be examined. Is the assertion supported by a model or by known facts? Does it make sense? By sharing the justification for assertions, students learn to trust their ability to understand mathematics.

> *Example:* What number comes next? What is your reason?
>
> 1, 1, 2, 3, 5, 8, 13, . . .

4. *Mathematical connections:* The power of mathematics to solve real-world problems, as well as problems in curricular areas other than mathematics, may be illustrated in many ways. Lessons that "connect" in significant ways help students to conceive of mathematics as a whole rather than as isolated tasks.

> *Example:* Write a paragraph describing how you would keep a record of the growth of a flower from a seed to a mature plant.

5. *Estimation:* Students must be trained when and how to estimate. By using estimation in a wide variety of situations, students can link conceptual and procedural knowledge and begin to appreciate the question "Is that answer reasonable?"

> *Example:* A handful of seed corn is spread evenly over the surface of a checker board. Estimate the number of seeds on the board by using the number of seeds on one square of the board.

6. *Number sense and numeration:* The development of a reliable number sense and an accurate concept of numeration is basic to the development of mathematical concepts and procedural thinking.

> *Example:* **You are given 156 beans. How many piles of 10 beans can you make?**

7. *Concepts of whole number operations:* Before students can become effective problem-solvers, they must develop a meaningful concept for each of the basic operations and recognize that differrent problem situations imply the use of different mathematical operations.

> *Example:* **Shade an area of a piece of graph paper to represent the operation 8 × 3.**

8. *Whole number computation:* Paper-and-pencil computation, calculators and computers, and mental arithmetic and estimation are all basic skills in a technological society. Students must be able to do all three types of computation and know when each type is called for.

> *Example:* **At the store, Mrs. Smith used her calculator to determine the total cost of 19 apples costing 40 cents each. She obtained the answer $5.60. Is this answer reasonable?**

9. *Geometry and spatial sense:* Students need to develop spatial sense and the ability to represent objects by using language, models, and diagrams. The classification of two- and three-dimensional objects, their measurement, and the ways that they embody various mathematical concepts are all topics of great importance.

> *Example:* **Using a geoboard, create an object having five sides and five angles. Is there more than one such object?**

10. *Measurement:* Measurement links the abstractions of mathematics with real-world problems. Students should become familiar with the concepts of length, capacity, weight, area, volume, time, temperature, and angle as modeled in everyday objects and events, and make measurements and estimates to the nearest unit of these quantities.

> *Example:* **If you want to measure the length of your foot, would you prefer to use a unit of length which is shorter than your foot or longer than your foot. Why?**

11. *Statistics and probability:* Students should be taught to collect, organize, and describe data as well as interpret displays of data. The concept of chance should also be explored.

> *Example:* **Make a display that will show which kind of milk the children in your class prefer: white or chocolate.**

12. *Fractions and decimals:* Students need to develop a number sense about fractions and decimals that integrates with their sense of the whole numbers. The importance of fractions and decimals in real-life problem solving should be emphasized.

> *Example:* **Given a piece of graph paper, shade an area to represent the decimal .3. Next, shade an area to represent the fraction $\frac{1}{4}$. Which area is greater?**

13. *Patterns and relationships:* Students need to learn to recognize, describe, and create a wide variety of patterns involving numbers and geometrical objects, and to represent the patterns as mathematical relationships.

> *Example:* **Find the next three numbers in this sequence: 5, 9, 13, 17, 21, . . .**

Goals for 5–8 Mathematics

The broad goals of the curriculum for grades five through eight are the same as for the K–4 curriculum: to help students learn the value of mathematics, become confident of their ability to do mathematics, become mathematical problem-solvers, communicate mathematically, and reason mathematically.

To meet these goals, the NCTM makes the following assumptions about classroom materials:

- Every classroom will have ample supplies of manipulative materials (See Chapter 5).

- Teachers and students will have access to appropriate resource materials from which to develop problems and ideas for explorations.

- All students will have an appropriate calculator.

- Every classroom will have at least one computer available at all times for demonstrations and student use.

The curriculum standards for grades five through eight extend the K–4 standards and introduce new topics and challenges.

1. *Mathematics as problem solving:* Students extend their set of problem-solving strategies and apply them in the solution of multi-step problems. They verify and interpret results and generalize solutions and strategies to other problems and thus gain confidence as problem-solvers.

> *Example:* There are nine students in a school club. How many different pairs of students could act as representatives of the group in a student senate? What if there were 12 students in the group?

2. *Mathematics as communication:* Students represent problems using oral, written, concrete, pictorial, graphic, and algebraic methods, and develop common understandings of mathematical ideas by using the skills of reading, listening, and viewing to interpret mathematical ideas. Students also discuss mathematical ideas and make conjectures.

> *Example:* Represent the following instructions using algebraic expressions:
> Pick a number.
> Multiply it by itself.
> Subtract four.
> Divide by two less than the original number.

3. *Mathematics as reasoning:* Students should learn to apply deductive and inductive reasoning to a wide variety of problems, and to make use of spatial reasoning, proportional reasoning, and graphs in problem solving. Making and testing conjectures and evaluating the arguments of others reveals the role and power of reasoning in mathematics.

> *Example:* A student asserts that, "If you multiply two primes, you get another prime." How would you support or challenge this statement?

4. *Mathematical connections:* Students should see mathematics as a system of thought that offers important insights and problem-solving skills in many curricular areas and in life. By exploring practical problems involving graphic, numerical, physical, algebraic, and verbal mathematical descriptions, students will see the importance of mathematics to our society.

> *Example:* A Forest Service map is scaled so that one inch on the map represents 200 feet in reality. If a new trail 2350 feet long is added, how long should the trail line be on the map?

5. *Number and number relationships:* Students need to understand and use numbers in a variety of equivalent forms (fractions, decimals, percentages, exponential and scientific notation, and so on). Ratio and proportion, percent, fractions, and decimals should be applied in many different situations.

> *Example:* Find two fractions equivalent to the decimal 4.1.

6. *Number systems and number theory:* The purpose of this standard is to help students develop an understanding of our number system as a whole and to apply number-theory concepts (primes, factors, common multiples, and so on) in real-world problem-solving situations.

> *Example:* Give an example of a geometrical problem for which an irrational number is the only answer.

7. *Computation and estimation:* Use paper-and-pencil calculation, mental arithmetic and estimation, and calculators and computers on problems involving whole numbers, fractions, decimals, and percents. Develop and explain methods for using proportions in problem-solving.

> *Example:* Estimate the height in feet of a stack of one million dollar bills.

8. *Patterns and functions:* Students will describe, analyze, extend, and create a wide variety of patterns, representing the patterns by using tables, graphs, and rules. They will also examine functional relationships, using patterns and functions to solve problems.

> *Example:* How many diagonals can be drawn in a regular hexagon? A regular octagon? A regular *n*-gon? Make a table and look for a pattern.

9. *Algebra:* Students need to understand the concept of a variable, an expression, and an equation, and to use these concepts to represent patterns and functions.

> *Example:* Given the following data, write an equation relating the number N to the number M.
>
> | N | 3 | 4 | 5 | 6 |
> |---|---|---|---|---|
> | M | 7 | 9 | 11 | 13 |

10. *Statistics:* Students should systematically collect, organize, and describe data, by using tables, charts, and graphs. They also need to make inferences and support conjectures based on data analysis, and to evaluate the arguments and inferences of others.

> *Example:* Explain why very small samples may produce misleading statistics.

11. *Probability:* Students need experience simulating probability models and talking about their interpretation. The point is to provide students with experiences that show the value of probability as a means of understanding events in the real world.

> *Example:* A student states that the odds of obtaining heads on the tenth flip of a series of coin flips somehow depends on what happened on the preceding flips. How would you react to this statement?

12. *Geometry:* Students need to identify, describe, compare, and classify objects and to relate these objects to problems in the real world. They should also explore transformations of geometric figures.

> *Example:* Collect three natural objects that exhibit some form of symmetry. Sketch the objects and draw in any lines of symmetry or points for turn symmetries.

13. *Measurement:* Students extend their concept of measurement to include derived and indirect measurements like speed, and so forth, and use measurement as a tool in problem solving.

> *Example:* Measure the distance around your classroom by using the following three instruments: a 6" ruler; a yardstick; and a measuring tape. Discuss the differences between the three answers you obtain. Which instrument do you think provided the most accurate answer? Why?

PLANNING FOR IMPROVEMENT

Mathematics education in America must change. The only way for that to happen is for individual teachers to change what they teach and the way they teach. To accomplish this, they will need the support of the public and school administrators at all levels.

Finding the motivation and conviction for such a task is the first step. All interested parties should be encouraged to read the reports summarized in this chapter and to study the recommendations of the NCTM *Curriculum and Evaluation Standards*. Teachers should examine their own teaching practices in light of these recommendations and should ask themselves: "What do you emphasize? How do your students experience mathematics?—as a series of lectures or as an ongoing dialogue, with themselves as participants? Are you a vessel-filler or a lamp-lighter?" Administrators should examine the support they give to mathematics education and the criteria they use when evaluating teachers and student progress.

Teachers and administrators should enlarge their own professional growth programs to include regular reading of the mathematics education literature; participation in state, regional, and national mathematics education conferences; and ongoing dialogue with other teachers and administrators at the district level. Mathematics education specialists at many universities and state education departments are available for consultation. These individuals can help orient your district's parents, teachers, and administrators to the problems in mathematics education, and provide information resources to help your district make well-founded plans and decisions.

SUMMARY AND CONCLUSIONS

According to many studies of mathematics achievement, American students are "majoring in minors;" they spend too much time drilling on paper-and-pencil-computation and too little time learning how to use mathematics as a tool. One result of this emphasis is that American students consistently perform at or below international averages on standardized measures of overall mathematics achievement. The same studies indicate that the root of this problem lies in a curriculum which fails to expose American students to the range of mathematics experienced by their international peers.

The National Council of Teachers of Mathematics publication *Curriculum and Evaluation Standards for School Mathematics* (1989) provides a detailed outline of a K–12 mathematics curriculum that addresses the curricular problems facing American mathematics education. However, the question remains, "Will the standards significantly change the way that mathematics is taught in America?" Only a small proportion of elementary school teachers and administrators belong to the NCTM. Even fewer school board members belong. In the end, mathematics teaching will only change when the textbook publishers change the texts that, in America, define the mathematics curriculum.

However, in spite of the difficulties involved, concerned teachers, administrators, and parents can make a difference in solving this problem. Share your concerns with other teachers and parents. Discuss the NCTM standards. Insist that the school board support local efforts to implement the NCTM standards. Join the NCTM and get involved in state and national dialogues. If enough people follow this advice, publishers will respond with new books. Administrators and school boards will raise their expectations and level of support. Mathematics education in America will improve.

DISCUSSION QUESTIONS

1. The new NCTM standards focus on problem solving and concept development. Review the topics at the K–4 and 5–8 grade levels. Which topics do you feel prepared to teach? Which are you unprepared to teach? Discuss your concerns with other teachers and administrators in your school district, with the goal of planning a series of inservice days dealing with the mathematics curriculum.

2. In *Everybody Counts*, students, teachers, parents, administrators, and state and national leaders are urged to become involved with the reform of American mathematics education. Review the recommendations listed in the section entitled "Leadership" in this chapter. Do you think the leaders in your community would respond to an invita-

tion to discuss mathematics education? Share the recommendations with other professional educators. Plan a public meeting that will involve local parents, business leaders, and government officials. Find out who is willing to help and how.

3. What do your students think of mathematics? Do they think it is important, or do they think mathematics is a waste of time? What can you do to show them the value of mathematics?

4. What do your students' parents think of mathematics? Do they value it? What can you do to help parents to understand the importance of mathematics and share that perception with their children?

SUGGESTED READINGS AND REFERENCES

Crosswhite, F. Joe, et al. *Second International Mathematics Study: Summary Report for the United States.* Washington, DC: National Center For Educational Statistics, 1985.

Crosswhite, F. Joe, et al. *Second International Mathematics Study: Detailed Report for the United States.* Champaign, IL: Stipes, 1986.

Dossey, John, et al. *The Mathematics Report Card: Are We Measuring Up?* Princeton, NJ: Educational Testing Service, 1988.

Kilpatrick, Jeremy. *Academic Preparation in Mathematics: Teaching for Transition From High School to College.* New York: College Entrance Examination Board, 1985.

McKnight, Curtis C. *The Underachieving Curriculum: Assessing U.S. School Mathematics from an International Perspective.* Champaign, IL: Stipes, 1987a.

McKnight, Curtis C. Report prepared for the fall 1986 meeting of the Mathematical Sciences Education Board. Quoted on p. 6 of *The Underachieving Curriculum.* Champaign, IL: Stipes, 1987b.

National Commission on Excellence in Education. *A Nation at Risk: The Imperative for Educational Reform.* Washington, DC: U.S. Government Printing Office, 1983.

National Research Council, Board on Mathematical Sciences. *Everybody Counts: A Report to the Nation on the Future of Mathematics Education.* Washington, DC: National Academy Press, 1989.

National Science Board, Commission on Precollege Education in Mathematics, Science, and Technology. *Educating Americans for the 21st Century.* Washington, DC: National Science Foundation, 1983.

Working Groups of the Commission on Standards for School Mathematics of the National Council of Teachers of Mathematics. *Curriculum and Evaluation Standards for School Mathematics.* Reston, VA: National Council of Teachers of Mathematics, 1989.

CHAPTER 4

The Differences We See among Children

How shall we regard our differences? Should we ignore them or acknowledge them? If we acknowledge them, should we view our differences with suspicion or treat them as a resource? In either event, to what extent should public education accommodate individual differences? If American education cannot or should not address individual differences, where does individuality figure in the curriculum?

These questions are important, far-reaching, and troubling. This chapter begins by asserting that we must acknowledge our differences and look for ways to interpret those differences positively, treating them as human resources rather than as troubling liabilities. By developing a diverse pool of human talent and potential, we strengthen our national readiness for whatever challenges may come, both anticipated and unforeseen. In so doing, we give individual children the opportunity to be the very best they can be within the confines of their limitations.

This chapter addresses the issue of individual differences as they pertain to mathematics education. For instance, how do differences in learning style affect what happens in school? How can parents and teachers use an understanding of these differences to improve student achievement and attitudes toward mathematics? Why do women and ethnic minorities appear to abandon the study of mathematics so early in their high school education? What are the consequences of this exodus? What can be done to encourage women and minorities to continue their mathematics education?

DIFFERENT TYPES OF PEOPLE

Do people come in various "types"? In recent years, the notion that observations of human behavior can be used to classify people into various personality types has become popular. The reasons for the popularity of such classification schemes are straightforward. First, human behavior is complex and may be somewhat bewildering to the casual observer. Classification schemes help to simplify the observation and interpretation of human behavior. Second, they are supported by our past experiences with people. All of us have met people who, though unrelated, share an amazing variety of expressions, habits, values, and ambitions. So in a sense, formal classification schemes tend to give substance to a host of informal impressions and hunches formed over the years.

Having agreed that classification schemes are convenient, we must also recognize that few researchers believe that the different categories of personality types or learning styles correspond to actual biological or psychological differences in individuals. All such classification schemes are far too simple and limited in scope to adequately describe human behavior. However, they are useful in that they allow us to study various aspects of human behavior without becoming overwhelmed.

Different Learning Styles

What is a "learning style"? Basically, a learning style is nothing more than a person's habitual approach to perception and thinking. For instance, some people are more perceptive than others, noticing sounds, sights, and smells which others fail to sense. Some people are remarkably perceptive of the emotional states of others; such people are often sympathetic and may be known as "good listeners." Other individuals may appear blind to anybody's feelings but their own. In any event, people clearly vary in the degree to which they "tune in" to the world and the people around them.

With respect to differences in thinking, all of us have friends who regularly appear to appreciate the soundness of our thinking and arguments. Equally, all of us know a few people who persist in challenging our arguments, values, and agenda whenever they get the opportunity. They can look at the same problem we see and come up with a totally different analysis. In fact, sometimes we may have a very difficult time following their thinking! Therefore, different people clearly have different thinking styles.

Gregorc's Learning Styles Model

In a natural extension of this approach to understanding human behavior, Anthony Gregorc (1979) developed a classification scheme that characterizes differences in learning styles. In Gregorc's model of learning styles, two factors describe each individual's approach to learning.

The first factor considered is the degree to which a person prefers a step-by-step approach to life. For example, one person may demand order in everything she or he does. Tasks are taken up one at a time, carried to completion, then checked for accuracy. Only after a task is completed will this type of person begin another. For such people, called *sequential* thinkers by Gregorc, there is a place for everything and everything must be in its place.

By contrast, some other people are bored by order and feel confined by routine. These people, called *random* thinkers by Gregorc, prefer to work on several tasks simultaneously. For such individuals, it is more satisfying to begin several tasks at once, alternating between them until all are completed. For these people, variety is the spice of life.

Gregorc's second factor addresses the extent to which people prefer concrete, hands-on experiences more than abstract thinking. A person who prefers working with things to working with ideas is called a *concrete* thinker. Such thinkers are often recognized for their practical approach to life.

By contrast, other people prefer to work with ideas. Gregorc calls this type of person an *abstract* thinker. These individuals prefer to work with ideas, creating not things but theories, plans, and new insights.

Gregorc's model combines these four characteristics to form four categories of learners: concrete sequential; abstract sequential; abstract random; and concrete random.

What Is Your Learning Style?

Using criteria developed by Kathleen Butler (1987) and Anthony Gregorc, you can determine your own learning style. For instance, if you are naturally well-organized, if you judge value according to practicality, if you feel you have met the challenge of the day when you have something to show for your time, if you are task-oriented, if you relax by puttering and fixing things, and if people praise your reliability and accuracy, you may be a concrete sequential learner.

On the other hand, you might be an abstract sequential learner if you tune in regularly to documentaries on television, love the world of ideas and research, consider yourself a thinker or idea specialist, use your creative energies to develop new ideas or explanations of natural phenomena, and if others see you as an analytical and intellectual thinker.

If you regard emotions, the arts, and relationships as the real stuff of life, you may be an abstract random learner. You may also avoid competition and regard relationships more highly than accomplishments.

Finally, if you are a natural inventor, you may be a concrete random learner. If so, you march to a different drummer, seeing things differently than most people and using that trait to create or refine products and processes in new ways.

An Example of Different Learning Styles

The following example illustrates the way that an understanding of Gregorc's model of learning styles can help to explain misunderstandings between adults.

Larry Logical is an office manager for a medium-sized insurance firm. Because of his natural organizational skill, he has made a name for himself among his colleagues as a thorough, dependable manager. The efficiency of Larry's department is also a common topic of discussion among Larry's administrative superiors. Everyone knows that Larry is on the way up in the company.

Larry was a model worker even as a child. School papers were turned in complete and on time. Writing assignments were models of neatness. Indeed, it troubled Larry when teachers returned his manuscripts with appreciative comments scrawled across the page. Larry preferred a simple "A" in the margin on the first page. It looked "cleaner" somehow.

Each evening, Larry's wife, Mary Metaphoric, studies the arrangement of the various components of their evening meal before calling her family to supper. The table setting is always as much a delight to the eye as the food is to the palate.

Mary's artistic flair was greatly appreciated by her teachers. Her exuberant, intuitive, and imaginative contributions in school added color to many classroom discussions and extracurricular activities. Mary's teachers also knew her to be a girl who needed both to give and receive tokens of approval. She liked to see comments scrawled on her returned manuscripts. She also felt the need to discuss the big questions in life. Mary was and still is an idealist.

Larry's and Mary's problem didn't surface in a way that permitted easy identification. In fact, Larry didn't sense any trouble at all. It was Mary who felt a lack of something.

At first, she reproved herself for being petty; husbands do slip out of the role of suitor. Small courtesies and tokens of love give way to a more mundane routine.

Eventually, however, she felt short-changed. Take yesterday, for instance. Larry walked in the door and began an inspection of the house: clothes on the floor in the bedroom, dishes in the sink, a pile of newspaper clippings on the table, and no supper in sight.

What had Mary been doing all day? The implication that she wasn't doing her share hurt Mary and she snapped back with a comment of her own, calling Larry cold and unsympathetic. Mary had spent the day visiting a lonely neighbor in need of some company. Mary counted the time well spent. Larry grumbled something about priorities and sank into his chair to read the paper. That evening, they began to talk about the argument and Mary's sense that something was wrong.

If you were sitting in on their discussion, could you offer help without taking sides? One way to do so would be to explain the concept of learning styles, using Gregorc's model, and help them to see the effect that differences in their learning styles have on their perceptions of the problem and its causes.

Using Gregorc's model of learning styles as the basis for an analysis of the problem, let's assume that Larry Logical is a concrete sequential thinker and that Mary is an abstract random thinker.

Recall that concrete sequential thinkers are highly sensitive to disorder and feel a need to put things in their proper places. Also, concrete sequential thinkers are not particularly aware of the emotional states or needs of those around them, hence Larry's unintentional "blindness" to Mary's emotional unrest and need for regular tokens of reassurance.

On the other hand, Mary's alertness to her neighbor's emotional needs prompted her to answer that need as best she could. To Mary's thinking, answering the needs of a lonely neighbor takes precedence over housework. However, in ignoring the housework, she unintentionally offended Larry, implying by her action that she rejects his sense of priorities and personal need for order in the home.

What is the solution to the problem? For starters, both Larry and Mary need to recognize the limitations in their own thinking and perception. Then they need to understand each other's needs and priorities, accepting that neither position is perfect and that both have legitimate ways of being. Finally, they both need to begin anticipating each other's needs and feelings.

Learning Styles in School

If an understanding of learning styles can improve relationships between adults, think what this concept could mean in an educational setting, which is exactly the point of Kathleen Butler's book *Learning and Teaching Style In Theory and Practice* (1987).

After reviewing Gregorc's theory of learning styles, Butler discusses the implications of this model for both students and teachers. Perhaps the most significant issue that she raises relates to a problem faced by most teachers: How to allow students the freedom to demonstrate their learning in a manner that takes advantage of each student's strengths, while still maintaining high expectations of scholarship.

Butler's principal concern is that teachers, being normal people like Larry Logical and Mary Metaphoric, are apt to structure their lessons, assignments, and evaluations in such a way that only those students who share the teacher's learning style can really perform at their best. In such a situation, students with learning styles different from that of the teacher are likely to experience frustration, without being able to say why.

For instance, if an English teacher is concrete sequential, she or he is apt to be very concerned with the formal aspects of written and spoken communication: grammar, spelling, punctuation, diction, and so forth. Assignments would be likely to stress form rather than substance, freedom of expression, and emotional content. Written essays would probably be the way in which students were asked to demonstrate their mastery of analysis and communication.

On the other hand, an abstract random English teacher would probably be less interested in the formal aspects of written and spoken communication than in the degree to which his or her students engage the issues and emotions which form the substance of a piece of literature. To accomplish this end, an abstract random teacher might rely more on panel discussions, skits, and speeches for evaluating the extent of a student's understanding of a story or issue.

We can easily appreciate the plight of an abstract random student in a concrete sequential teacher's class. Longing for debate, role-playing, and other demonstrative activities, the student endures an endless sequence of drill, essays, and lectures. Even highly motivated students can be bored stiff in the face of such frustration.

Similarly, a concrete sequential student in the class of an abstract random teacher is apt to sense a lack of clear purpose in all the activity. After all, such students want to perfect well-defined skills and master specific content information. The lack of focus on such goals can lead a concrete sequential student to feel that he or she is not really learning anything useful.

Applying these thoughts to a mathematics classroom, a concrete sequential teacher is apt to focus on skill development and the memorization of facts and procedures. Such teachers have the tendency to apply knowledge rather than discuss its meaning, to see detail rather than generalizations, and to be right-answer- oriented rather than process-oriented. At this point, concrete sequential readers are thinking, "right on!" However, other readers are thinking, "And what of the beauty of mathematics? What of its meaning? When do the students get the big picture? That teacher can't see the forest for the trees!"

Are these criticisms valid? Yes, if you can accept the premise that mathematics is more than computation and memorization. University mathematicians, famous for being somewhat random in their ways, would be quick to point out that the real purpose of learning mathematics is not to do by hand what calculators do quickly and accurately, but to use mathematics to understand the world. That requires both skill and understanding.

A child growing into an abstract random learning style could be systematically deprived of what she or he most needs by a steady diet of concrete sequential mathematics. Conversely, a concrete sequential child looks for order and predictability in mathematics. Generalizations and alternative thinking are low on such a child's agenda. Imagine the frustration of such a child in the class of an abstract random teacher. All the time the teacher is developing an appreciation for the meaning of some concept, the child just wants to know how to *do* it.

Different Strokes for Different Folks

Butler's book provides a remedy for parents and teachers willing to follow the same advice that Larry and Mary need: discover the needs and priorities of those around you, accept their differences as legitimate, and find ways to accommodate the needs of a variety of learners. After all, we no longer force naturally left-handed children to write with their right hands. Is it any less a mistake to force children consistently to demonstrate their understanding in ways that they find intellectually clumsy and emotionally unsatisfying?

Parents can begin by recognizing that the differences they see in their children may require different kinds of support. One child's notion of mathematics may be radically different from another's. Little concrete sequentials can grow up to be accountants and CPA's. Little abstract sequentials can grow up to be scientists. Both use mathematics, but in different ways. Part of a parent's task is to help each child find the best and most natural use of his or her talents. Teachers can begin by studying the needs of children with various learning styles. Then they should plan alternative activities and assignments to bring out the very best their students have to give.

In approaching this challenge, Butler's book offers practical advice and examples in a wide variety of curricular areas. Figures 4.1–4.4, reprinted from Butler's book, show the relationship between Bloom's

FIGURE 4.1   The Concrete Sequential Style

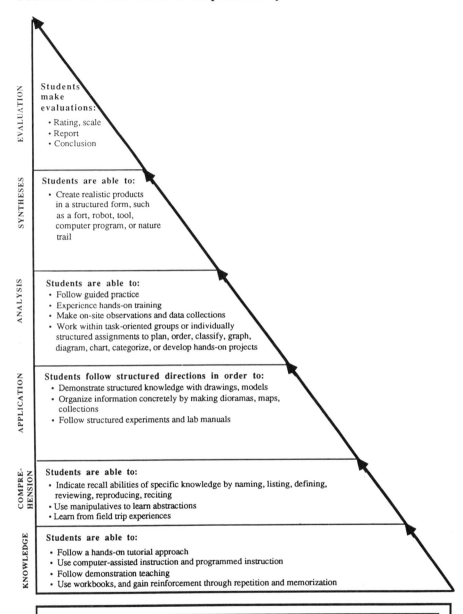

EVALUATION

Students make evaluations:
• Rating, scale
• Report
• Conclusion

SYNTHESES

Students are able to:
• Create realistic products in a structured form, such as a fort, robot, tool, computer program, or nature trail

ANALYSIS

Students are able to:
• Follow guided practice
• Experience hands-on training
• Make on-site observations and data collections
• Work within task-oriented groups or individually structured assignments to plan, order, classify, graph, diagram, chart, categorize, or develop hands-on projects

APPLICATION

Students follow structured directions in order to:
• Demonstrate structured knowledge with drawings, models
• Organize information concretely by making dioramas, maps, collections
• Follow structured experiments and lab manuals

COMPRE-HENSION

Students are able to:
• Indicate recall abilities of specific knowledge by naming, listing, defining, reviewing, reproducing, reciting
• Use manipulatives to learn abstractions
• Learn from field trip experiences

KNOWLEDGE

Students are able to:
• Follow a hands-on tutorial approach
• Use computer-assisted instruction and programmed instruction
• Follow demonstration teaching
• Use workbooks, and gain reinforcement through repetition and memorization

The Concrete Sequential Style: Levels of Student Performance

Reprinted with permission of the copyright holder, Kathleen A. Butler, Ph.D.

FIGURE 4.2 The Abstract Sequential Style

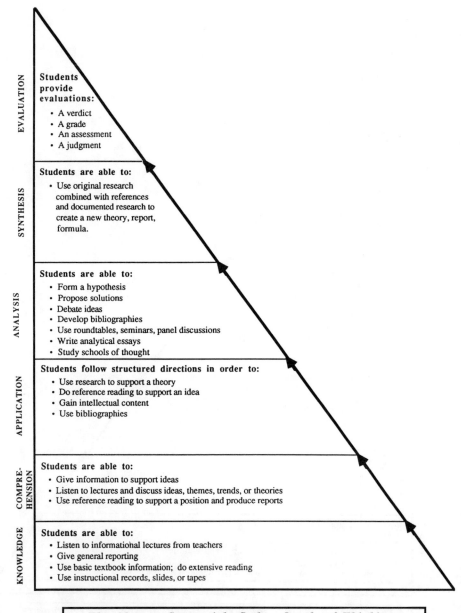

EVALUATION

Students provide evaluations:
- A verdict
- A grade
- An assessment
- A judgment

SYNTHESIS

Students are able to:
- Use original research combined with references and documented research to create a new theory, report, formula.

ANALYSIS

Students are able to:
- Form a hypothesis
- Propose solutions
- Debate ideas
- Develop bibliographies
- Use roundtables, seminars, panel discussions
- Write analytical essays
- Study schools of thought

APPLICATION

Students follow structured directions in order to:
- Use research to support a theory
- Do reference reading to support an idea
- Gain intellectual content
- Use bibliographies

COMPRE-HENSION

Students are able to:
- Give information to support ideas
- Listen to lectures and discuss ideas, themes, trends, or theories
- Use reference reading to support a position and produce reports

KNOWLEDGE

Students are able to:
- Listen to informational lectures from teachers
- Give general reporting
- Use basic textbook information; do extensive reading
- Use instructional records, slides, or tapes

The Abstract Sequential Style: Levels of Thinking

Reprinted with permission of the copyright holder, Kathleen A. Butler, Ph.D.

94

FIGURE 4.3   The Abstract Random Style

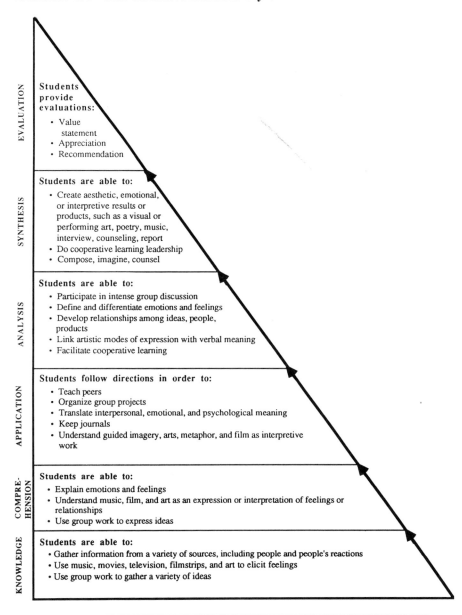

EVALUATION

Students provide evaluations:
- Value statement
- Appreciation
- Recommendation

SYNTHESIS

Students are able to:
- Create aesthetic, emotional, or interpretive results or products, such as a visual or performing art, poetry, music, interview, counseling, report
- Do cooperative learning leadership
- Compose, imagine, counsel

ANALYSIS

Students are able to:
- Participate in intense group discussion
- Define and differentiate emotions and feelings
- Develop relationships among ideas, people, products
- Link artistic modes of expression with verbal meaning
- Facilitate cooperative learning

APPLICATION

Students follow directions in order to:
- Teach peers
- Organize group projects
- Translate interpersonal, emotional, and psychological meaning
- Keep journals
- Understand guided imagery, arts, metaphor, and film as interpretive work

COMPRE-HENSION

Students are able to:
- Explain emotions and feelings
- Understand music, film, and art as an expression or interpretation of feelings or relationships
- Use group work to express ideas

KNOWLEDGE

Students are able to:
- Gather information from a variety of sources, including people and people's reactions
- Use music, movies, television, filmstrips, and art to elicit feelings
- Use group work to gather a variety of ideas

The Abstract Random Style: Levels of Thinking

Reprinted with permission of the copyright holder, Kathleen A. Butler, Ph.D.

95

FIGURE 4.4 The Concrete Random Style

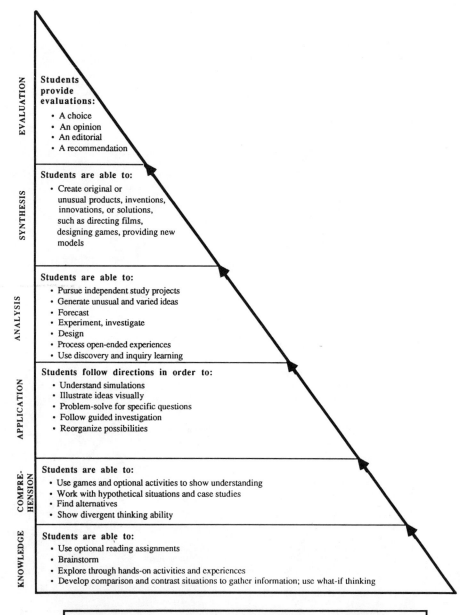

The Concrete Random Style: Levels of Thinking

Reprinted with permission of the copyright holder, Kathleen A. Butler, Ph.D.

96

taxonomy of the cognitive domain and the different learning styles. These figures illustrate in general terms the variety of approaches that may be taken in assigning tasks at the six levels of Bloom's taxonomy: knowledge, comprehension, application, analysis, synthesis, and evaluation.

The challenge for mathematics teachers is to use Butler's approach to create alternative learning and evaluation tasks for specific units of instruction. Teachers should not feel obligated to create a variety of tasks at each level of the cognitive domain for each learning style. Although a comprehensive set of tasks might evolve naturally over a period of years, a reasonable beginning could involve creating a limited set of options focusing on the higher levels of Bloom's taxonomy. For example, a sixth-grade teacher planning a unit on addition and subtraction of unlike fractions might offer four options for the following unit project.

> **Your task is to make up and solve a word problem that requires either addition or subtraction of unlike fractions. (Extra credit if it requires both!) Be prepared to present your problem to the class and answer questions.**
>
> **For concrete sequential students: You may prepare a poster illustrating the problem and showing the steps in your solution.**
>
> **For abstract sequential students: You may represent the problem using manipulatives and explain your solution in a report.**
>
> **For abstract random students: You may describe the problem, act it out, and demonstrate your solution.**
>
> **For concrete random students: You may perform an experiment that will give you the answer, then demonstrate the experiment to the class.**

Each of these options offers students a slightly different opportunity, yet the basic task is the same for all: create and solve a complex problem using the concepts, media, and presentation skills that give them the best chance to shine. Providing students with this type of freedom to be the very best they can be is the goal of style-based instruction.

WOMEN AND MATHEMATICS

"What's a nice girl like you taking mathematics for?" Spoken or implied, most female students can expect to encounter this question in some form if they continue their study of mathematics past the junior year in high school. Is it really so unnatural or unusual for a female to study advanced mathematics? Are boys somehow better-suited to mathematics than girls? The following discussion examines these and other related questions.

A Brief Comparison of Male and Female Achievement in Mathematics

What do we know about the mathematics achievement of males and females? In elementary school, in the few areas where differences in mathematics achievement exist, girls tend to outperform boys, particularly on arithmetic computation tasks. This advantage in computation appears to persist throughout elementary, junior high, and high school.

In junior high, about half of the observable differences in achievement tend to favor girls. The other differences favor the boys. A rather startling difference that shows up at this age is in the relative number of boys and girls scoring at the highest levels on standardized achievement tests oriented to secondary-level mathematics. For example, in a study of junior high students given the SAT college entrance test (Meer 1984), for every girl scoring 700 or higher (out of 800 possible points), 13 boys achieved comparable scores.

In high school and college, most of the observable differences in mathematics achievement favor the males, especially differences related to problem-solving tasks requiring higher-level mathematical reasoning.

Before reaching any conclusion about what a difference in achievement scores means, it may be instructive to think about what a comparison of male and female achievement involves. For the sake of this discussion, assume that the measure of achievement used in making the comparison is the mathematics portion of the Scholastic Aptitude Test (SAT).

The SAT tests little in the way of mathematics taught below the seventh grade. Instead, it emphasizes secondary-level mathematics and mathematical reasoning. Clearly, if the SAT measures the extent to which students have mastered secondary-level mathematics and how successfully they solve problems requiring the type of reasoning practiced in those courses, students with four years of high school mathematics will have some advantage over students with only one or two years of study beyond the eighth grade.

In general, females tend to take fewer high school mathematics courses than males. Females are also more apt to be found in lower-level mathematics courses (Campbell 1986). Conversely, males take advanced courses more frequently than females. This trend is also true for science and computer courses. Since males tend to take more mathematics than females, one would expect the males to outperform the females on the SAT, which is exactly what happens.

If males' SAT scores are separated from females' scores, it will always be seen that males' scores range from very low, below 100, to a perfect score of 800. Females' scores do the same, although, once again, more males than females typically score above 700. Since neither the spread in scores nor the achievement of the very best students is a suitable indicator of the overall performance of high school seniors, some other basis is needed for the comparison of males' and females' mathematics achievement. Normally, the arithmetic average, or mean, has been used for this purpose.

Before a great deal is made of the difference between the average scores of males and females, the size of the difference should be considered relative to the spread in the scores. The basic question should be "How big is the difference between the groups' averages compared to the differences that exist within each group?" For instance, suppose that in some year, the average SAT score for males turns out to be 490 points and the females' average turns out to be 450 points. Does this 40 point difference mean that most high school males are smarter than most high school females when it comes to mathematics? Certainly not. In order to state that most males outperformed most females, the difference between the group averages would have to be much larger in comparison to the differences that exist within each group. This is not the case in the example or in real life.

So what do the differences mean? The differences obtained are statistically significant, which means that they are probably real. That is, high school males apparently know more mathematics than high school females. Nevertheless, a lot of females still score higher than the "average" male. The difference between the average scores is much less than the differences occurring among either the girls or the boys.

Why the Differences?

Why do females perform lower on the SAT mathematics exam than males? There may be several reasons, one or more of which may be based on differences in development between boys and girls. However, there are enough brilliant female mathematicians to persuade anyone that any such gender factors cannot be the principal reason behind the differences in mathematics achievement on the SAT. The main reasons are probably to be found in the different treatment that females receive in mathematics classes and in society in general.

The real effect of that differential treatment begins to show about the time children enter junior high. A number of studies (Campbell 1986) have investigated the importance that males and females attach to mathematics and their expectations of success in mathematics courses. In general, the findings of those studies show that, beginning at about the junior high level, both boys and girls tend to think of mathematics as an activity that is socially more suitable for males than for females. Also at this age, among boys and girls of equal ability, the boys tend to express higher expectations of success in mathematics than do the girls.

Any parent with teenagers knows that the junior high years are a time of intense personal examination for children. As they ponder the changes in their bodies and emotions, teenagers also begin looking for indications of the man or woman they will ultimately become. Generally, they are worried about whether they will grow up to be "normal." One of the ways they cope with the stress and insecurity of not knowing whether they will turn out all right is to formulate a self-image which is ultra-masculine or ultra-feminine: anything to avoid ambiguity. Theirs is an age of overstatement and exaggeration; all the hyperbole is just part of the smokescreen covering their insecurity.

In such an emotional climate, the boys are looking for an identity that is truly masculine. Traditionally, mathematics has been a male-dominated domain. Females who take advanced courses in mathematics represent two threats to the males. First, they increase the competition. Second, by being in the course, they hint that the boys' choice of course may not be all that masculine after all. The boys will not appreciate either implication and will communicate their feelings either directly or indirectly, including the implication that real girls don't belong in trigonometry—and, by the way, real boys only date real girls.

In the face of such opposition, it takes a girl with a clear sense of who she is and what she wants to persist in taking trigonometry. Even if she does enroll in an advanced course, will her teacher treat her the same as the boys? At both the elementary and secondary levels, mathematics teachers tend to initiate more contact with boys than with girls. They also tend to ask more difficult questions of the males (Campbell 1986). At the high school level, teachers often provide males and females with different types of feedback: girls receive commendation for their participation and cooperation; boys are challenged to support their answers and try harder. In effect, such teachers are telling the girls, "Nice try. I know you did your best," and the boys, "Try again. I know you can do better." Small wonder that females tend to lose confidence in their math ability and then give up on mathematics. Small wonder that they also look to other disciplines in which they might seek an education and a career.

A Few Consequences

What are the consequences of the perception that mathematics is a male domain? First, among college-bound high school students, males more commonly take four years of mathematics than do females. As a result, female college students are less prepared to study the "hard" sciences, engineering, and mathematics than are male students. Today, only about 5 percent of the nation's practicing engineers and scientists are women.

Very few students who enter college with deficiencies in mathematics manage to catch up with the help of remedial mathematics courses. The vast majority of such students spend a year trying to prepare themselves for calculus, only to discover that the task is too difficult. Since calculus is a requirement for most scientific and technical curricula, these students must change their career plans and opt for some other field.

There is only one way for parents to save their children this frustration. If your children are planning on going to college, insist that they take as much high school mathematics as they can. Two years of mathematics is not enough for college-bound students. Since tenth-graders may not yet be mature enough to decide that they will not go to college, parents should not hesitate to insist that children continue their mathematics education beyond the minimum graduation requirements of the local high school.

For Your Consideration

A number of resources are available for parents and teachers to consult about the issues surrounding women in mathematics. Some of these publications also contain activities that parents can share with their children to encourage the study of mathematics. The following books are recommended:

Brush, Lorelie, et al. *Encouraging Girls in Mathematics: The Problem and the Solution.* Cambridge, MA: Abt Books, 1980.

Chipman, Susan, et al. *Women and Mathematics: Balancing the Equation.* Hillsdale, NJ: Lawrence Erlbaum Associates, 1985.

Skolnick, Joan, et al. *How to Encourage Girls in Math & Science.* Englewood Cliffs, NJ: Prentice-Hall, 1982.

Schildkamp-Kundiger, Erica. *An International Review of Gender and Mathematics.* Columbus, OH: ERIC Clearinghouse for Science, Mathematics, and Environmental Education, 1982.

MINORITIES AND MATHEMATICS

The record of achievement among many minority groups in mathematics and the sciences is also cause for concern. Of the nation's 2.7 million scientists, only 1.5 percent are black. Native Americans and Hispanics make up an even smaller component of our country's pool of scientists and engineers (Campbell 1986). These proportions are also reflected in the number of minority students earning doctoral degrees in mathematics and the physical sciences. For instance, in 1988, out of approximately 800 Ph.D.'s in mathematics, 4 went to black Americans, and 5 went to Hispanic Americans (Jackson 1989).

If comparisons are made between the standardized test scores of white students and those from racial minorities other than Asian Americans, the differences obtained are even greater than the differences between male and female students discussed earlier. From the middle of elementary school on, mathematics achievement test scores of whites are higher than those of blacks or Hispanics. These differences increase as the students grow older. Asian students score the highest of all racial or ethnic groups.

Looking at Differences

The reasons behind these differences are unknown, although opinions are plentiful. Certainly one component of the differences is related to bias introduced by the tests themselves. Most standardized achievement tests are written with a particular cultural orientation: white middle-class society. Black, Hispanic, and Native American students reading such an examination may be placed at a disadvantage on certain parts of the test where these cultural biases play a hidden role. On the other hand, mathematics is probably as "culture-free" as any discipline can be, so this factor is probably not an adequate explanation for the lower performance of non-Asian ethnic minorities. As in the case of female students, the main reason minorities achieve less in mathematics is probably that they study less mathematics.

Another significant factor may involve parental expectations. Parents affect their children's attitude toward mathematics in many ways. For instance, non-Asian American mothers tend to attribute success in mathematics to ability; Asian mothers everywhere attribute success in mathematics to effort (Peterson 1987). As a result, if a non-Asian American parent has the idea that mathematical ability does not run in the family, the parent is less likely to encourage the child to strive for high achievement in mathematics. By contrast, an Asian parent is apt to insist on a total commitment from the child to learn mathematics. Is it any wonder the Asian children outperform others? All parents should take pains to motivate their children.

Students influence one another by participating in discussions of values, career plans, and stereotyping. If minority students are not aware of the opportunities open to them as mathematicians, scientists, and engineers, they may not place much importance on the study of mathematics. Even if minority students are aware of these opportunities, however, there is always the concern that she or he could end up the only black engineer in a company of 1000 employees. The isolation implied in such a career scenario may pose serious problems for a young person planning a career.

Schools influence students in a multitude of ways. For instance, if the school climate is negative, and if students skip school regularly, students are more apt to achieve less and elect fewer mathematics courses. Poorly equipped, overcrowded, and run-down schools fail to motivate minorities or any other students to study mathematics. The presence of faculty role models is important as well. Just by being in the classroom, minority mathematics instructors of all races substantiate the assertion that success in mathematics is a matter of talent and hard work, not skin color or religious preference. To minority students who have never had a nonwhite mathematics teacher, the experience of having a minority mathematics teacher as a role model may lead some students to reevaluate their assumptions regarding their career options.

Suggestions for Parents and Teachers

Minority parents and teachers wanting to encourage students in the study of mathematics may find the following suggestions helpful. First, appeal to the students' natural inquisitiveness, and encourage them to explore and discover mathematics. Make these explorations relevant and conduct them in a socially enjoyable format. Minority students may separate their social and academic lives completely. Show them how they can have a good time while learning mathematics in a group. Second, discuss minority role models, such as black mathematicians and Native American scientists. Find articles and books that highlight the careers of these people and encourage students to think of themselves as capable of similar achievement. Third, make use of hands-on manipulative materials when developing concepts. Find interesting applications of the mathematics you teach. Fourth, encourage minority students to plan a sequence of high school mathematics classes. Point out the many jobs that require skills in mathematics and encourage the students to strive for excellence, not just remediation. Communicate with parents, helping them plan their child's high school program. Do not assume that minority students should automatically enroll in vocational education. Look for the minority students who could have a future in a technical field.

MATH ANXIETY

Most mathematicians have experienced the following scene at a party or a meeting. The mathematician is introduced to a confident and competent adult who says that he is a musician. On learning that he is speaking to a mathematician, his face falls, and he starts to stammer something about his frustrations and failures with mathematics. The mathematician feels no compulsion to excuse his profound inadequacies as a musician. The brief discussion ends with both parties feeling awkward and a bit foolish. Fifteen minutes later, the mathematician goes through the same scene with a French teacher.

Some people are terrified of mathematics. Faced with a mathematical task which ought to be routine, they freeze up, unable to think about anything but their perceived inability to cope with the problem. This anxiety affects millions of Americans to various degrees. It is called math anxiety, math avoidance, or fear of figuring.

How It All Begins

For some people, the foundation of math anxiety begins in elementary school with a simple yet incorrect assumption: the really important thing in mathematics is to get the right answer. This assumption is often reinforced by teachers who have a highly concrete sequential orientation to teaching. To such teachers drill and practice on math facts and procedures are the appropriate means for developing fluency with math facts, and accuracy and speed with paper-and-pencil computation.

The problem with this perception of mathematics is that it places little value on meaning and concept development. Instead, memorization becomes the tool for learning how to do mathematics. At first, this may not appear to be a particular problem, especially for the child with a good memory. However, as students pass through the grades, mathematics becomes more complicated, as previously encountered concepts are related to new concepts and processes. For the unfortunate child attempting to learn mathematics by memory, all of these concepts and processes, both old and new, seem unrelated. Each fact, each concept, each process must be stored in memory as a separate and distinct entity.

Sooner or later, children learning mathematics by memorization face a situation not unlike that encountered by a player building a house of cards. The child's capacity to select the correct item from an ever-growing host of seemingly unconnected options is stressed to the limit. Just like the house of cards, children's confidence in their ability to do mathematics comes tumbling down in a crushing realization that they somehow "missed the boat" years ago and are now hopelessly behind.

Once this terrible realization takes hold of a person, mathematics can only offer terror and shame. When true "mathophobes" sit down to a mathematics test or task, they quickly stop focusing on the task, regardless of how easy or difficult it may be, and sink into gloomy contemplation of their perceived inadequacies.

In addition to the scenario presented above, other experiences can cause people to begin to doubt their capacity to do mathematics. Even well-grounded students can suddenly find themselves in the dark if a key concept is missed or if a teacher plows through the material without concern for what the students understand or don't understand. Children caught in such circumstances need the understanding and help of their parents in dealing with their frustrations and in obtaining the academic help and relief they need.

Whatever the causes of math anxiety, parents and teachers should look at it as a serious problem and seek ways to help their children obtain the help they need. If left unattended, the problem may grow to paralyzing proportions and severely limit children's future career options.

A Remedy

Math anxiety is often built on years of misunderstanding. For some, it takes years, and possibly a lifetime, to conquer. If you, a friend, or a loved one are afflicted with math anxiety, you can ease the hurt and correct the misunderstanding. Begin by understanding that the problem is definitely not something for which the sufferer must accept blame. Assigning blame is both pointless and inappropriate.

Next, talk the problem over with other people who are math-anxious. Hearing their stories will reassure everyone involved that the problem has common roots and that definite steps can be taken to deal with the problem and its consequences. Find out if there is a math anxiety support group in your community. Such groups are common in college and university towns.

Finally, begin a study of the problem. Of all the resources available on the topic, Tobias' book *Overcoming Math Anxiety* (1987) is the most helpful. In it, Tobias discusses a number of strategies for dealing with the problem and developing a better self-image.

SUMMARY

Clearly, we are not all identical. We do not all approach the problems and tasks of life with the same perspectives and insights. One of the purposes of education is to help individuals recognize and develop their unique talents, for their own well-being and for the benefit of society. By accommodating a variety of learning styles, teachers can offer students an opportunity to explore ideas confidently and to demonstrate mastery of concepts and processes in ways that make use of their preferred modes of expression.

Beyond elementary school, women and most minorities perform lower on standardized mathematics achievement tests than white males and Asian-Americans. Women and non-Asian minorities take less mathematics than white males in high school and college. As a result, women and non-Asian minorities rarely enter professions requiring advanced study in mathematics, such as science, engineering, and mathematics.

All arguments about ability aside, no significant improvement in this situation will take place until more women, blacks, Hispanics, and Native Americans elect to continue their mathematics education. Counseling them in this direction is a direct step in dealing with this problem. Such counseling may require help with the problem of math anxiety, which affects millions of children and adults. Counseling may also involve helping students to redefine their study habits to include social study groups and other group support activities.

DISCUSSION QUESTIONS

1. What is your learning style? Do you feel that your learning style shapes your teaching? How does it affect what you expect of yourself? Your students? Plan a mathematics lesson that offers students options based on different learning styles. After you have taught the lesson, ask your students how they felt about having options. Did they think it was fair? Would they want to do it again?

2. Some people feel that female students experience subtle cultural pressures in mathematics classes and that these pressures tend to discourage women from taking advanced courses or from competing aggressively against male mathematics students. How do you feel about this accusation? Do you feel that it has any merit or do you feel it is untrue? Talk to several adults regarding their personal opinions and experiences with regard to this issue. If you believe that there is some truth to the accusation, what do you think your school district can or should do in response?

3. Asian students outperform all other groups in American mathematics education. Do you think that America should attempt to imitate Asian schools? Do you think American parents have a role to play in motivating their children to do well in school?

4. Math anxiety: do you think it is a learned behavior, a genetic defect, or just an excuse? How anxious are you about mathematics? Do you have any students who are math-anxious?

SUGGESTED READINGS AND REFERENCES

Bloom, Benjamin S. *Taxonomy of Educational Objectives. Handbook 1: Cognitive Domain.* New York: Longmans, Green, 1954.

Butler, Kathleen A. *Learning and Teaching Style in Theory and Practice,* rev. ed. Columbia, CT: The Learner's Dimension, 1987.

Campbell, Patricia B. "What's a Nice Girl Like You Doing in a Math Class?" *Phi Delta Kappan,* vol. 67, no. 7 (March 1986), 516–519.

Gregorc, Anthony F. "Learning/Teaching Styles: Their Nature and Effects." In *Student Learning Styles, Diagnosing and Prescribing Programs*. Reston, VA: National Association of Secondary School Principals, 1979.

Jackson, Allyn. "Minorities in Mathematics: A Focus on Excellence, Not Remediation." *American Educator* (Spring 1989).

Meer, Jeff. "Mathematical Gender Gap: Narrowing or Inborn?" *Psychology Today*, vol. 18, no. 3 (March 1984), 76–77.

Peterson, Ivars. "Education: Math and Aftermath." *Science News*, Vol. 131, No. 5 (Jan. 31, 1987).

Tobias, Sheila. *Overcoming Math Anxiety*. Boston: Houghton-Mifflin, 1987.

CHAPTER 5

Enriching Mathematics Learning

Teachers and parents can do much to enrich the mathematical learning of children. Manipulative materials, activity cards, video and film productions, computer software, books, and a host of other instructional supports are available. This chapter will identify several resources and make recommendations regarding their use.

MANIPULATIVE MATERIALS

The following materials are recommended for teaching a wide variety of concepts in the K–8 mathematics curriculum: attribute materials, pattern blocks, numeration materials, and geoboards. Most of these materials may be constructed, with some effort and a few dollars for supplies. Commercially produced manipulatives and activity guides are also available from mail-order supply houses.

A partial list of suppliers willing to mail a free catalog to inter-

111

ested teachers and parents appears at the end of this chapter. For the purpose of illustrating the variety of materials available, the following abbreviations will be used to designate a few of the mail-order suppliers of educational materials for mathematics: Cuisenaire Company of America, Inc. (C); Creative Publications (CP); Dale Seymour Publications (DS); Spectrum Educational Supplies, (S); Delta Education (DE); Educational Teaching Aids (ETA); Nasco (N); Sunburst Communications (SC); International Business Machines (IBM); Minnesota Educational Computing Consortium (MECC); Houghton Mifflin (HM); Addison-Wesley (AW).

Attribute Materials

Attribute materials generally take the form of a set of geometric objects in different sizes, shapes and colors. For example, a typical set might contain each of the following objects in three colors and two sizes: equilateral triangles, squares, rectangles, and circles. Such a set would consist of twenty-four objects, no two of which are identical. Teachers often manufacture sets of attribute materials themselves by cutting the objects out of poster board. A basic template for these shapes is given in Figure 5.1.

These objects are primarily used for teaching students to recognize the various features of geometrical objects and to sort the materials on the basis of similarities and differences. This may ultimately lead to discussions of various hierarchial sorting schemes, part-whole thinking, and investigation of statements making use of the qualifiers "all," "some," "none," and so forth.

The following examples illustrate two tasks that may be investigated by using attribute materials.

Task #1 Sort all of the objects into two piles. In the first pile, place the objects which are either red or not triangles. All the others go into the second pile.

Task #2 The purpose of this task is to create a "chain" of objects, each differing from its two adjacent objects by exactly one attribute. Working in groups of three or four, place a starting object on the table. Then take turns adding one object at a time to the "chain." Repeat the general procedure, changing the rule to "The number of differences between adjacent objects is two." Then try

FIGURE 5.1   Attribute Materials

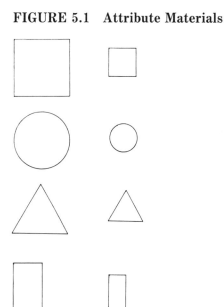

three differences. Repeat, changing the rule so that there is exactly one similar trait between adjacent objects. Is one similarity the same as two differences?

Both tasks provide ample opportunities to develop language and logical skills. Teachers may elect to approach these tasks in whole-group discussion using colored acetate figures on an overhead projector, or in small groups using teacher-made or commercial materials. In either setting, the focus should be on logic and language, not on getting any particular answer.

Several commercially produced activity books are available to guide discovery and foster insight when using attribute materials:

1. ESS Program at EDC in Boston, *Attribute Games and Problems, ESS Teacher's Guide.* Grades K–6. (DE)
2. Martha Marolda, *Attribute Games and Activities.* Grades K–8. (S) (CP)

3. Don Balka, *Attribute Logic Block Activities.* Grades 2–6. (DS) (C) (CP)
4. Judy Goodnow, *Moving on with Attribute Blocks.* Grades 4–6. (CP) (S)

Pattern Blocks

Pattern blocks normally consist of a set of geometrical objects having the property that the pieces may be fitted together in certain ways without gaps or overlap. This property is guaranteed by using objects having only two possible edge lengths, one twice the other, and by using only certain angles. The objects are often color-coded, each shape having a different color. A template for making your own pattern blocks is shown in Figure 5.2. A typical set might contain the following objects: 24 hexagons, 24 squares, 48 triangles, 48 trapezoids, 48 parallelograms, and 48 rhombuses.

In using these blocks, children are free to create appealing designs, all of which tile (cover) the plane. Of course, many mathematical

FIGURE 5.2 Pattern Blocks

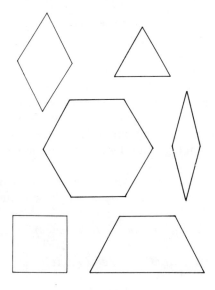

discoveries can be made. The following tasks illustrate some of the possibilities.

> *Task #1:* Given a silhouette of a geometrical object, find a pattern block design that will exactly cover the silhouette.
>
> *Task #2:* Find a pattern block design that will cover an area by using only triangles and squares. Is there more than one possible design? Try using only parallelograms and triangles.
>
> *Task #3:* Using pattern blocks, create an object that, by itself, will tessellate (cover without gaps or overlaps) the plane.
>
> *Task #4:* Use pattern blocks to investigate the perimeter of a geometrical object that can be covered with a pattern block design, using one of the blocks' two possible edges as a unit of length.

As with the attribute materials, pattern blocks offer many opportunities for language development. In addition to this, many interesting mathematical questions may be asked, and many satisfying answers can be found. Several commercially produced activity books are available for teachers and parents to use in guiding discovery and building insights. For example,

1. Marian Pasternack and Linda Silvey, *Pattern Blocks Activities*. Grades K–9. (DS) (C) (S) (DE) (N)
2. Sandra Mogenson and Judy Magarian-Gold, *Pattern Animals Book*. Grades 1–4. (C) (ETA)
3. Arthur Wiebe, *Symmetry with Pattern Blocks*. Grades 3–9. (C) (S) (DE) (ETA)
4. Creative Publications, *Hands on Pattern Blocks*. Grades K–3. (CP) (S)
5. Matthew E. Zullie, *Fractions with Pattern Blocks*. Grades 2–6. (CP)

Numeration Materials

The use of numeration materials, sometimes called base-ten blocks, is discussed in chapter 1 in some detail. Unlike the two-dimensional, teacher-made materials illustrated in Figure 1.3, commercially produced numeration materials are normally three-dimensional, with a small cube serving as the unit called "chip." A "strip" is a row of ten small cubes, and a "flat" is a ten-by-ten array of chips. A ten-by-ten-by-ten cube is used to represent one thousand. Thus, the commercially produced materials offer the student four columns of objects to manipulate.

The following books provide activities based on numeration materials:

1. Mary Laycock, *Base Ten Mathematics*. Grades 2–8. (DS) (N) (C)

2. *Base Ten Block Activity Book*. Grades 2–5. (N) (ETA)

3. Elsie Robertson, Mary Laycock, and Peggy McLean, *Skateboard Practice–Addition & Subtraction*. Grades 1–3. (DE) (C)

4. Peggy McLean and Mary Laycock, *Skateboard Practice–Multiplication & Division*. Grades 3–6. (DE) (C)

5. Creative Publications, *Hands On Base Ten Blocks*. Grades K–3. (S) (CP)

6. Micaelia Randolph Brommett and Linda Holden Charles, *Understanding Place Value–Addition & Subtraction*. Grades 2–6. (S)

7. Linda Holden Charles and Micaelia Randolph Brommett, *Understanding Place Value–Multiplication & Division*. Grades 2–6. (S)

8. Evelyn Neufeld and James S. Lucas, *Number-Blox Activities–Books A and B*. Grades K–6. (CP)

9. Robert Willcutt, Carole Greenes, and Mark Spikell, *Base Ten Activities*. Grades K–6. (CP)

10. Rebecca S. Nelson, *Games and Activities with Base Ten Blocks–Books One and Two*. Grades 1–4. (C)

Geoboards

Geoboards have been used for a number of years to teach geometrical concepts such as area and perimeter and to represent various arithmetic operations with whole numbers and fractions. Figure 5.3 shows a

FIGURE 5.3   Geoboard

typical geoboard: a five-by-five array of finishing nails spaced about one inch apart on a piece of wood with smooth edges. Teachers may arrange for class sets of geoboards to be constructed by shop students or supportive parents. Each child in class should have a geoboard. Commercially produced geoboards are normally made of plastic. Both types of geoboards act as grids on which geometrical objects are defined by stretching rubber bands over nails or plastic tabs.

The following tasks illustrate some of the uses of geoboards:

Task #1: Construct the following objects:
A square four units on a side.
A square with area of four square units.
A rectangle with area of two square units.
An octagon (eight-sided figure).
A trapezoid (four-sided figure with only two sides parallel) with area of seven square units.

Task #2: Construct squares having the following length (See Activity 8 in Chapter 8):
Square root of two.
Square root of five.
Square root of ten.

Task #3: Construct squares having the following area:
Two.
Five.
Ten.

Task #4: Represent the following using the geoboard:
$\frac{1}{3}$ (of some object)
$\frac{2}{5} * \frac{1}{4}$

Task #5: Find a formula (Pick's Rule) that will give you the area of any polygon created on the geoboard by counting the nails on the border of the polygon and the number of nails in the interior of the polygon.

The following commercial materials support the use of geoboards:

1. Charles Lund, *Dot Paper Geometry-With or Without Geoboards.* Grades 4–8. (C) (S) (DE) (ETA) (N) (DS)

2. Alan Barson, *Geoboard Activity Cards-Intermediate Set.* Grades 3–8. (C) (CP)

3. Alan Barson, *Geoboard Activity Cards-Primary Set.* Grades 1–3. (CP)

4. Margaret Farrell, *Geoboard Geometry.* Grades K–12. (CP)

5. Creative Publications, *Hands On Geoboards.* Grades K–3. (CP) (S)

6. Shirley Hoogeboom, *Moving On with Geoboards.* Grades 4–6. (CP) (S)

7. John Bradford, *Geoboard Teacher's Manual.* Grades K–12. (DS)

8. John Trivett, *Introducing Geoboards.* Grades K–3. (DS)

FILMS AND VIDEO MEDIA

In addition to materials in print, a limited number of high-quality video and film resources are available for mathematics educators. The following resources are specifically oriented to elementary school mathematics:

Burns, Marilyn. *Mathematics with Manipulatives.* A series of six videotapes illustrating the use of base-ten blocks, pattern blocks, cuisenaire rods, color tiles, geoboards, and six models. Professional development and product promotion. Includes a teacher discussion guide. (C) (S)

Burns, Marilyn. *Mathematics for Middle School.* Focuses on teaching problem solving in grades 6–8. Professional development and product promotion. Includes a teacher discussion guide. (C)

The Challenge of the Unknown. A seven-part film series, focusing on problem-solving in the real world, produced by Phillips Petroleum Company, Bartlesville, OK. Available from Karol Media, 22 Riverside Drive, Wayne, NJ 07470–3191. A teaching guide is available from W.W. Norton and Company, Inc., 500 Fifth Ave., New York, NY 10110.

Square One Television. Produced by Children's Television Workshop. Half-hour programs, aired Monday through Friday on most PBS stations. Aimed at the nation's 14 million eight- to twelve-year-olds. For a program guide and teacher's guide, write to Square One Television, Children's Television Network, One Lincoln Plaza, New York, NY 10023.

The Geometric Supposer Video and *The Supposer in the Classroom Video.* Professional development and product promotion. Free 30-day loan. (SC)

The Voyage of the Mimi. Twenty-six 15-minute videotape programs available in BETA or VHS. Related computer programs, student workbooks, and teacher's guide. Free 30-day loan of overview of the series entitled, "What is the Voyage of the Mimi?" Grades 4–6. (SC)

MICROCOMPUTER SOFTWARE

Elementary school mathematics teachers have a wide variety of software to choose from. Some software, such as LOGO, provides "thinking environments" in which children build concepts and solve complex problems. Much software is designed to provide drill and practice in basic skills. Knowing when and how to use these resources is not easy. The following discussion focuses on "thinking environment" software, since such resources are typically the most exciting to students and are versatile tools for use in many grades. By contrast, drill and practice software is usually focused on a particular grade and sometimes a particular textbook series.

LOGO and Geometry

Several commercial versions of the LOGO language include Krell LOGO, Terrapin LOGO, Apple LOGO, IBM LOGO, Commodore LOGO, Atari LOGO, and LOGOWRITER. An excellent user-supported version of LOGO is also available through the PC Software Interest Group (PC-SIG), called Ladybug LOGO. This version of LOGO runs on IBM-compatible microcomputers and includes a manual on disk. Since PC-SIG disks cost approximately $6.00 each, this version of LOGO offers students and teachers with access to IBM-compatible microcomputers an inexpensive opportunity to try LOGO. The address for PC-SIG is in the section of software sources at the end of this chapter.

The following books support LOGO activities:

1. Margaret Moore, *LOGO Discoveries.* Available in Terrapin/Krell or Apple LOGO formats. Grades 3–12. (CP)

2. Margaret Moore, *Geometry Problems for LOGO Discoveries.* Available in Terrapin/Krell or Apple LOGO formats. Grades 5–12. (CP)

3. Margaret Moore, *LOGO Discoveries Series with Teacher Resource Disks.* Available in Terrapin/Krell or Apple LOGO formats. Grades 3–12. (CP)

4. *LOGO Works: Great Problems in LOGO. For Atari LOGO.* Grades 5–12. (N).

The following software packages offer student and teacher a convenient environment in which to study the features of geometrical objects.

1. *The Geometric Supposer Series:*
   Judah L. Schwartz and Michal Yerushalmy, *Points and Lines.* Grades 5-12.
   Judah L. Schwartz and Michal Yerushalmy, *Triangles.* Grades 8-12.
   Michal Yerushalmy and Richard Hoode, *Quadrilaterals.* Grades 8-12.
   Judah L. Schwartz and Michal Yerushalmy, *Circles.* Grades 8-12. (SC)

2. Educational Development Center, *Elastic Lines: The Electronic Geoboard.* Grades 2-8. (SC)

3. WICAT Systems, Inc., *The IBM Geometry Series: Geometry One.* Grades 8-12. (IBM)

General Problem-Solving and Calculators

General mathematical problem-solving involves a host of skills. The following computer programs offer interactive environments for the development of select problem-solving skills and concepts.

1. Doug Felt et al., *In Search of the Secret Stone: A mathematics Problem-Solving Adventure.* Concepts, skills, and problem solving. Grades 4-9. (CP)

2. Thomas C. O'Brien, *Winker's World of Patterns.* Pattern recognition involving numbers, colors, and words. Grades K-6. (SC)

3. Thomas C. O'Brien, *Blockers and Finders.* Problem-solving, logic. Grades 1-12. (SC)

4. Thomas C. O'Brien, *Safari Search.* Problem-solving, logic. Grades 3-12. (SC)

5. Thomas C. O'Brien, *The King's Rule.* Concepts, skills, problem-solving. Grades 4-12. (SC)

6. Marge Kosel and Mike Fish, *The Factory.* Problem-solving. Grades 4-12. (SC)

7. Mike Fish and Marge Kosel, *The Super Factory.* Problem-solving. Grades 6–12. (SC)

8. Thomas C. O'Brien, *The Royal Rules.* Concepts, skills, problem-solving. Grades 6–12. (SC)

9. Victoria Hanson and John D. Perron, *Recycling Logic.* Logic. Grades 6–12. (SC)

10. *Mirrors on the Mind—Strategy.* Problem-solving, logic. Grades 8–12. (AW)

11. *Mathematics: Solving Story Problems.* Problem-solving skills. Grades 3–6. (HM)

12. *Problem-Solving Strategies.* Problem-solving skills. Grades 5–9. (MECC)

13. *Gertrude's Secrets.* Problem-solving, logic. Grades K–3. (AW)

In addition to computer software, several activity books are available to teach the use of calculators.

1. Terrence G. Coburn, *Calculate! Problem Solving with Calculators.* Grades 3–8. (CP) (S)

2. George Immerzeel and Earl Ockenga, *Calculator Activities for the Classroom.* Grades 4–9. (CP)

3. Reys et al., *Keystrokes: Calculator Activities for Young Students.* Grades 2–8. (CP)

4. Don Miller, *Calculator Explorations and Problems.* Grades 5–12. (C)

5. Chuck Lund and Margaret A. Smart, *Focus On Calculator Math.* Grades 5–12. (C) (N)

6. Janet Morris, *How to Develop Problem Solving Using a Calculator.* Grades 7–12. (DS)

7. Terrence G. Coburn, *How to Teach Mathematics Using a Calculator.* Grades 2–8. (DS)

8. Terrence G. Coburn, Shirley Hoogeboom, and Judy Goodnow, *The Problem Solver with Calculators.* Grades 4–8. (S)

A BOOK FOR EVERY PURPOSE

The variety of support materials available in print is wide both in content and style. Choosing from among so many options is difficult enough for experienced buyers of such materials. Beginning teachers often have no idea what is available or what to expect from various authors and publishers.

The following pages, taken from a variety of books, are a far from representative sample of what is available. They do reveal the nature of activity books. No endorsement is implied. Table 5.1 identifies the sources of these materials, and each of Figures 5.4–5.12 is a sample of the materials in the particular series.

Table 5.1   Sources of Sample Pages

Figure	Source
5.4	*The Pattern Factory* (CP)
5.5	*Moving on with Pattern Blocks* (CP)
5.6	*Hands on: Base Ten Blocks* (CP)
5.7	*Reasoning with Dinosaur Counters* (CP)
5.8	*The Problem Solver 3* (CP)
5.9	*Thinker Tasks* (CP)
5.10	*Teaching Problem-Solving Strategies* (AW)
5.11	*Teaching Problem-Solving Strategies* (AW)
5.12	*LOGO Probability* (Terrapin)

FIGURE 5.4 Sample from *The Pattern Factory*

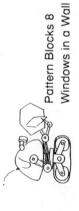

Pattern Blocks 8
Windows in a Wall

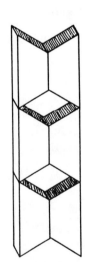

A wall with 1 window
takes 4 blocks to build.

A wall with 2 windows
takes 6 blocks to build.

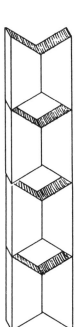

A wall with 3 windows
takes 8 blocks to build.

How many blocks to build a wall with 10 windows?

Windows	Blocks
1	4
2	6
3	8

The Pattern Factory
©1980 Creative Publications, Inc.

Reprinted with permission.

FIGURE 5.5   Sample from *Moving on with Pattern Blocks*

Finding multiple solutions for covering a figure   Name

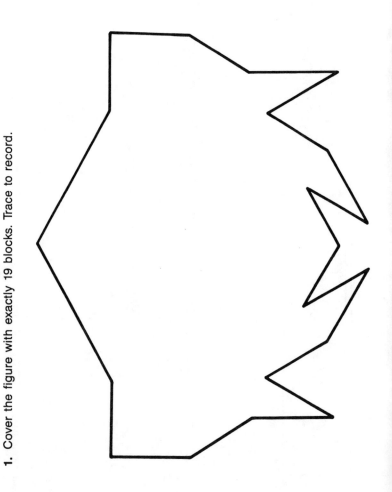

1. Cover the figure with exactly 19 blocks. Trace to record.

2. Now cover it with different groups of blocks. Record each group.

⬡	◀	◀	tan ╱	■	blue ◢	total

MOVING ON WITH PATTERN BLOCKS
© 1988 Creative Publications

Reprinted with permission.

127

FIGURE 5.6 Sample from *Hands on: Base Ten Blocks*

★★★★★★★★★★★
LET'S SOLVE IT!

NAME

Look at each group of blocks. Some blocks are hidden.
Look at the total value. What value is hidden?

1.

Total
Value ___34___

Hidden
Value _____

2.

Total
Value ___26___

Hidden
Value _____

3.

Total Value __47__

Hidden Value _____

4.

Total Value __36__

Hidden Value _____

Using clues to find solutions

Reprinted with permission.

HANDS ON: Base Ten Blocks, Book 2
©1986 Creative Publications

FIGURE 5.7 Sample from *Reasoning with Dinosaur Counters*

Story 21   Name _____

Surf's up! Lily Lizard is giving surfing lessons at the beach. There are green, red, and blue dinosaurs learning to balance themselves on surfboards. There are 28 dinosaurs in all. There are 4 more red dinosaurs than green dinosaurs. There are 3 fewer blue dinosaurs than green dinosaurs. How many dinosaurs of each color are trying to surf? Watch out for flying surfboards!

▲ Use dinosaurs to act out the story.

▲ Draw colored circles to show your work.

REASONING WITH DINOSAUR COUNTERS, GRADES 2–4
© 1989 Creative Publications

131

FIGURE 5.8 Sample from *The Problem Solver 3*

USE LOGICAL REASONING   Name _____

1 The Heebie-Jeebies are playing music in the lunchroom. Harry, Helen, Herman, and Harriet are in the band.

- Harry and Herman have ears.
- Herman does not have a nose.
- Harriet and Helen have hair.
- Helen has knobs on the top of her head.

What name belongs on each name tag?

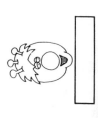

FIND OUT
- What is the question you have to answer?
- How many Heebie-Jeebies are playing in the band?
- What are their names?
- What do you know about Harry?
- What is one thing you know about Herman? What else do you know about him?
- What do you know about Harriet?
- What is one thing you know about Helen? What else do you know about her?

• Circle to show what you choose.

SOLVE IT • What does the first clue tell you? Look at the pictures on your paper. Which players could be Harry and Herman?

• What does the second clue tell you? Which of the two players is Herman? Write Herman's name on his name tag. Then who is the other player? Write his name on his name tag.

• What does the third clue tell you? How many players have hair? Who are those players?

• What does the fourth clue tell you? Which one of those two players is Helen? Write Helen's name on her name tag. Then who is the other one? Write her name on her name tag.

LOOK BACK • Look back to see if your answer fits with what the problem tells you and asks you to find. Read the problem again. Look back over your work. Does your answer fit?

The Problem Solver 3
Reprinted with permission.

FIGURE 5.9 Sample from *Thinker Tasks*

Name _____

Mystery Numbers 8

Read the clues for each mystery. Make lists of possible numbers that fit the clues. Find the mystery number.

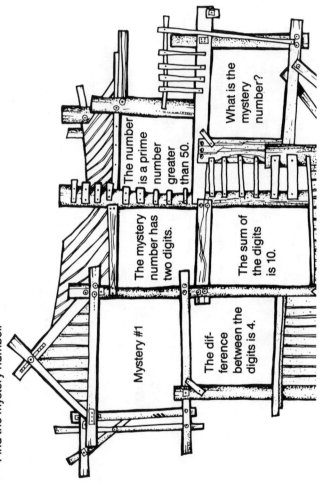

Mystery #1

The mystery number has two digits.

The number is a prime number greater than 50.

The difference between the digits is 4.

The sum of the digits is 10.

What is the mystery number?

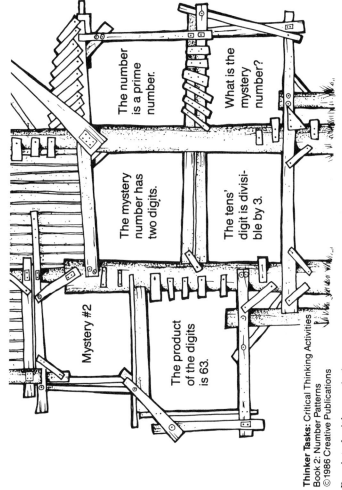

Mystery #2

The mystery number has two digits.

The number is a prime number.

The product of the digits is 63.

The tens' digit is divisible by 3.

What is the mystery number?

Thinker Tasks: Critical Thinking Activities
Book 2: Number Patterns
© 1986 Creative Publications

Reprinted with permission.

135

FIGURE 5.10 Sample from *Teaching Problem-Solving Strategies*

(Unit V ELIMINATION 81)

WORKSHEET 1—Solve by Elimination

1. Ace Detective Shamrock Bones of the City Homicide Squad is investigating a murder at the Old Grand Hotel. Five men are being held as suspects.

- "Giant Gene" Green. He is 250 cm tall, weighs 140 kg, and loves his dear mother so much that he has never spent a night away from home.

- "Yoko Red." He is a 200 kg Sumo wrestler.

- "Hi" Willie Brown. He is a small man only 130 cm tall; he hates high places because of a fear of falling.

- "Curly" Black. His nickname is a result of his totally bald head.

- Harvey "The Hook" White. He lost both of his hands in an accident.

Use the following clues to help Detective Bones solve this crime.

a. The killer was registered at the hotel.

b. Before he died, the victim said the killer had served time in prison with him.

c. Brown hair from the killer was found in the victim's hand.

d. The killer escaped by diving from the third floor balcony into the river running by the hotel and then swimming away.

e. Smudges were found on the glass table top indicating that the killer wore gloves.

2. Find the number described by the clues below. Circle the correct number.

   a. It is divisible by 4.
   b. It is larger than 8641.
   c. It is an even number.
   d. The sum of the digits is 21.
   e. It is less than 9756.

What does this eliminate? _____

Which clue(s) should you use first? _____

6552   9078   8948   9984   5483   9341   9714

     9096   9462   8643   8832   3242

          10341   2359

               1874   8706   8814

Reprinted with permission from *Teaching Problem-Solving Strategies* By Daniel T. Dolan and James Williamson.

137

FIGURE 5.11 Sample from *Teaching Problem-Solving Strategies*

(Unit III PATTERNS 39)

WORKSHEET 1—*What's Missing?*

Look at the sequences below and fill in the blanks so that your answers complete the Pattern.

1. 1, 4, 7, 10, ____, ____, ____, ____, 25

2. 0, 5, 10, 15, ____, ____, ____, ____, 40

3. 61, 57, 53, ____, ____, ____, ____, 33

4. 1 × 2, 2 × 3, 3 × 4, ____, ____, ____, ____, 8 × 9

5. 3, 6, 12, ____, ____, ____, 384

6. 1, 3, 6, 10, ____, ____, ____, 45

7. 101, 99, 96, ____, ____, ____, ____, 66

8. 2, 4, 8, ____, ____, ____, ____, 256

9. 720, 360, 120, ____, ____, ____, 1/7

10. 1, 4, 3, 6, 5, ____, ____, ____, 9, 12

Use the last term to check your Pattern.

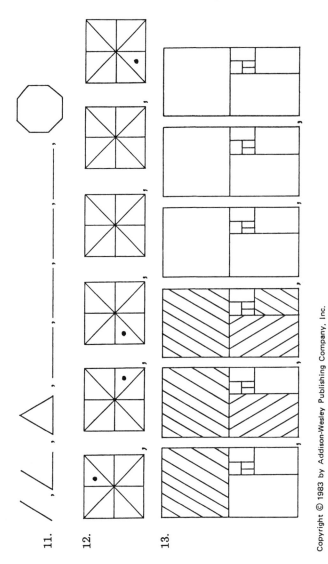

Reprinted with permission from *Teaching Problem-Solving Strategies* By Daniel
T. Dolan and James Williamson.

139

FIGURE 5.12   Sample from *LOGO Probability*

2 · A Random Walk

Imagine yourself in the middle of a city. You have no particular place to go, so you decide to walk randomly through the streets. To help you decide whether to turn right or left, you flip a coin at each intersection. If it turns up heads you go right and if it turns up tails you go left. What might your path look like?

To get a good idea of a possible path, you can define a procedure to have the Logo turtle simulate your journey by moving on the graphics screen.

Take some time to think about how you might define a procedure to do this.

• • •

One way is to write a recursive procedure like WALK:

```
TO WALK
FD 10
RIGHT.OR.LEFT
WALK
END
```

WALK calls the subprocedure RIGHT.OR.LEFT, which uses the result of FLIP to decide which way to turn:

```
TO RIGHT.OR.LEFT
IF FLIP = "HEADS THEN RT 90 ELSE LT 90
END

TO FLIP
OUTPUT PICK.ONE [HEADS TAILS]
END

TO PICK.ONE :OBJECT
OUTPUT ITEM (1 + RANDOM COUNT :OBJECT) :OBJECT
END
```

Reprinted with permission from *The LOGO Probability Student Booklet*, copyright by Terrapin Inc. 1988.

FIGURE 5.12 (Continued)

Define these procedures or read the file WALK from the Probability Disk.

Type DRAW, which starts the turtle at HOME, pointing straight up. Then type WALK and see what happens. Remember that at any time you can stop the procedure by pressing <CONTROL-G>.

Will the turtle ever find its way back to HOME?

Suppose the graphics screen is a city and the turtle is moving along the streets. Will the turtle eventually walk on every street in the city?

Experiment with the procedures. Try changing the angle the turtle turns in the procedure RIGHT.OR.LEFT to get some different results.

What angle would give you the most (or least) likely chance of getting back HOME?

Modify the procedure WALK to check whether or not the turtle has returned to its HOME position. HOME is located at the position (0,0) in the center of the graphics screen. In Logo, HOME can be referred to as the list [0 0]. You will find the following two procedures useful as tools.

```
TO HOME?
OUTPUT POSITION = [0 0]
END

TO POSITION
OUTPUT LIST XCOR YCOR
END
```

Edit WALK to include a line to test whether or not the turtle is at its HOME position.

• • •

Take some time to experiment with these procedures. Here are a few changes you can make in addition to your own ideas:

- change the inputs to RT and LT so that the angles are not both the same
- use PC 6 for an interesting effect
- change the angle inputs to RT and LT to RANDOM 360
- edit WALK so the turtle moves forward a random amount
- try a weighted coin

Reprinted with permission from *The LOGO Probability Student Booklet*, copyright by Terrapin Inc. 1988.

142

CONTESTS AND SCIENCE FAIRS

Hundreds of science fairs are held every year. Indeed, most western countries value the development of scientific talent very highly and provide opportunities for youngsters to exhibit projects and compete for awards. These competitions take place on local, state, regional, and national levels, and provide age-group judging so that even very young scientists can be recognized for their achievements.

In the United States, the easiest way to find out about science fairs in your area is to contact the National Science Teachers Association (1742 Connecticut Avenue NW, Washington, DC 20009). Another important agency to contact is Science Service (1719 N Street NW, Washington, DC 20036). Science Service administers several programs, including the International Science and Engineering Fair and the Westinghouse Science Talent Search.

Two books that deal with science fairs and mathematics projects are *Winning with Science: The Complete Guide to Science Research and Programs for Students*, by William S. Loiry (Sarasota, FL: Loiry Publishing, 1983) and *Math Projects for Young Scientists*, by David A. Thomas (New York: Franklin Watts, 1988).

Local schools frequently run their own science fairs. Such occasions offer students an opportunity to display math projects done in school and at home. Whether the projects take the form of geometrical models, studies of number patterns, secret code systems, computer programs, computer graphics, or any of a host of other possibilities, the development of mathematics projects and the public display and judging of the entries make a statement about the commitment of the school and its students to quality education.

For junior high students, the MATHCOUNTS competition attracts thousands of school entries every year. This annual event is sponsored by the National Society of Professional Engineers, the CNA Insurance Companies, the Cray Research Foundation, the General Motors Foundation, the National Council of Teachers of Mathematics, and NASA. In this competition, teams of students take part in a "college bowl" type of event. In 1989, MATHCOUNTS offered the following scholarships to its national winners: First Place, $10,000; Second Place, $6,000; Third Place, $4,000. Registration materials for state-level competitions are normally available in September and due in November of each year. For further information, write to Mathcounts Foundation (1420 King Street, Alexandria, VA 22314) or call (704) 684–2828.

Junior and senior high mathematics competitions are also sponsored by many state-level professional organizations, such as the Montana Council of Teachers of Mathematics. Teachers and parents may obtain the names of state contest directors by writing the National Council of Teachers of Mathematics (1906 Association Drive, Reston, VA 22091). These contests are advertised in junior and senior high schools every year, attracting both individual and team entries.

NAMES AND ADDRESSES

Teachers and parents interested in mathematics education may find the following resources helpful. No endorsements are stated or implied.

Suppliers of Manipulative Materials, Books, and Computer Software

Activity Resources Co., Inc.
P.O. Box 4875
Hayward, CA 94540

Addison-Wesley Publishing Co. (AW)
Jacob Way
Reading, MA 01867

Creative Publications (CP)
788 Palomar Avenue
Sunnyvale, CA 94086

Cuisenaire Company of America, Inc. (C)
12 Church Street, Box D
New Rochelle, NY 10802

DLM Teaching Resources
P.O. Box 4000
Allen, TX 75002

Delta Education (DE)
Box M, Math Department
Nashua, NH 03061–6012

Didax Educational Resources, Inc.
One Centennial Drive
Peabody, MA 01960

Educational Teaching Aids (ETA)
199 Carpenter Avenue
Wheeling, IL 60090

Gamco Industries, Inc.
P.O. Box 1862P1
Big Springs, TX 79721

Houghton Mifflin Publishing Company (HM)
1 Beacon Street
Boston, MA 02108

International Business Machines Corporation (IBM)
[Software For Education Catalog]
Department TR
101 Paragon Drive
Montvale, NJ 07645

Janson Publications, Inc.
222 Richmond Street, Suite 105
Providence, RI 02903

Learning Alternatives
1791 Elm Road
Warren, OH 44489

LEGO Systems, Inc.
555 Taylor Road
Enfield, CT 06082–3298

Minnesota Educational Computing Consortium (MECC)
3490 Lexington Avenue North
St. Paul, MN 55126

Nasco (N)
901 Janesville Avenue
Fort Atkinson, WI 53538

Scholastic Inc.
P.O. Box 7502
Jefferson City, MO 65102

Scott Resources
P.O. Box 2121B
Ft. Collins, CO 80522

Dale Seymour Publications (DS)
P.O. Box 10888
Palo Alto, CA 94303

Spectrum Educational Supplies, Ltd. (S)
125 Mary Street
Aurora, Ontario L4G 1G3
Canada

Summit Learning
P.O. Box 493
Ft. Collins, CO 80522

Sunburst Communications (SC)
39 Washington Avenue
Pleasantville, NY 10570-2898

Universal Education
Math Department
320 S. Eldorado
Mesa, AZ 85202

J. Weston Walch, Publisher
321 Valley Street
P.O. Box 658
Portland, ME 04104-0658

Professional Associations and Organizations

Association for Computers in Mathematics and Science Teaching
P.O. Box 2966
Charlottesville, VA 22902

> This organization publishes *Journal of Computers in Mathematics and Science Teaching.*

International Council for Computers in Education
1787 Agate Street
University of Oregon
Eugene, OR 97403

> This organization publishes *The Computing Teacher*, which regularly features ideas for teaching elementary school mathematics.

National Council of Teachers of Mathematics
1906 Association Drive
Reston, VA 22091

> The largest association of K–12 mathematics teachers in the United States. Publishes *The Arithmetic Teacher, The Mathematics Teacher, The Journal for Research in Mathematics Education,* an annual *Yearbook,* and many other booklets and monographs.

School Science and Mathematics Association
126 Life Sciences Building
Bowling Green State University
Bowling Green, OH 43403

> This association publishes *School Science and Mathematics.*

Young People's LOGO Association
1208 Hillsdale Drive
Richardson, TX 75081

> This association publishes *Turtle News* and the *LOGO Newsletter.*

Computer Software

Sources of LOGO

Apple LOGO
Apple Computer, Inc.
Cupertino, CA 95014

Atari, Inc.
1265 Borregas Avenue
Sunnyvale, CA 94086

Commodore LOGO
Commodore Computer
487 Devon Park Drive
Wayne, PA 19087

Digital Equipment Corp.
Maynard, MA 01754

IBM LOGO
International Business Machines Corporation
Department TR
101 Paragon Drive
Montvale, NJ 07645

Krell Software, Corp.
1320 Stony Brook Road
Stony Brook, NY 11790

Terrapin, Inc.
380 Green Street
Cambridge, MA 02139

TI LOGO II
Texas Instruments
P.O. Box 53
Lubbock, TX 79408

Software Reviews

Microgram
EPIE Institute
P.O. Box 620
Stony Brook, NY 11790

MicroSIFT
500 Lindsay Building
300 S.W. Sixth Avenue
Portland, OR 97204

School MicroWare Reviews
Dresden Associates
P.O. Box 246
Dresden, ME 04342

SOFTSWAP
333 Main Street
Redwood City, CA 94063

Sources of Public-Domain and User-Supported Software

Computer Solutions
P.O. Box 354
Mason, MI 48854

International Apple Core
P.O. Box 880338
San Francisco, CA 94188-0338

Multipath, Inc.
P.O. Box 395
Montville, NJ 07045

PC Software Interest Group (PC-SIG)
1030 E. Duane, Suite D
Sunnyvale, CA 94086

Pandora Software
P.O. Box 590
Clearfield, UT 84015

Public Brand Software
P.O. Box 51315
Indianapolis, IN 46251

The Public (software) Library
P.O. Box 35705
Houston, TX 77235-5705

Queue, Inc.
562 Boston Avenue
Bridgeport, CT 06610

Shareware Express
Box 219
San Juan Capistrano, CA 92693-0219

SUMMARY

Most elementary and junior high school students gradually develop a dislike for mathematics. Taught as an abstract paper-and-pencil exercise, the subject has little attraction. However, teachers and parents can begin to change this perception of mathematics by selecting discussion topics that are relevant to young people, and by teaching mathematics as an activity in a social context. This chapter identifies a number of print, film, and computer resources for teachers and parents willing to try something other than "Do the odd problems from 1–49."

DISCUSSION QUESTIONS

1. Suppose that for each of the next three years, you had $200 to spend on manipulative materials, activity books, and computer software. What would you buy first? How frequently would you use the things you buy? What would you get in the second year? In the third year? Compare your shopping list with that of another teacher at your grade level.

2. If you don't belong to the NCTM or one of its state affiliates, write for information about membership benefits, costs, publications, and conventions. How would membership in such an organization change your professional life?

3. Do you know how to use manipulative materials effectively? The *Mathematics With Manipulatives* videotape series will show you. Get a group of teachers, administrators, and parents together and use the tapes as a springboard for discussion.

4. How would you feel about using *The Challenge of the Unknown* or *Square One TV* in your classroom? Why?

CHAPTER 6

Computers, Calculators, and Mathematics

Imagine that you are attending a faculty meeting at a local elementary school. As the meeting begins, the principal rises, glances uncertainly at the teachers, and says, "This meeting of the elementary school faculty is now in session. The school district has decided to follow the recommendation of the state mathematics teachers' association to begin using computers and calculators regularly in all mathematics classes. The purpose of this meeting is to begin a discussion of what that decision might mean to us individually and collectively. The floor is open for discussion." As a teacher, how would you react to this announcement? What response would you expect from your colleagues? How would your school's mathematics curriculum change, if at all?

USING COMPUTERS AND CALCULATORS

Computers and calculators may be like avocados in this respect: people tend to either hate them or sing their praises. If you already use calculators and computers regularly for personal and professional business, you are unlikely to abandon these devices in favor of older technologies such as paper-and-pencil computation, mechanical adding machines, and manual typewriters. In spite of the problems encountered in learning to use complicated modern technologies, the benefits they offer most users far outweigh their liabilities.

Of course, if you are not currently a calculator and computer user, you may regard the new technologies with skepticism. Is a colleague struggling to learn word processing or some other complex computer-applications package? Perhaps your principal is hinting strongly that your turn is next. Under such circumstances, skepticism often evolves into apprehension, then outright resistance.

As a classroom teacher, to what extent are you obligated to participate in the computer revolution?

A Question of Professional Ethics

In examining the ethics and obligations implied in the question, "Should teachers be required to use calculators and computers regularly in all mathematics classes?", it may be helpful to consider a parallel situation in another profession. For instance, suppose that a group of physicians is debating the question, "Should all physicians in our clinic be required to learn the use of a new diagnostic procedure?" Suppose also that you use that clinic for all your routine medical services.

As a patient, you realize that not all the physicians will master the new diagnostic procedure with equal success. Inevitably, some will be more skillful than others, and a few physicians may already know the procedure. To offer high-quality service, the clinic might train some physicians in the use of the new procedure and ask them to take referrals from the other physicians. Of course, this approach will mean added delays and extra expenses for some patients. However, if the new diagnostic procedure is applicable in only a few cases, this delay may not be a matter of deep concern. Also, patients are free to change physicians if they are dissatisfied with the service.

On the other hand, if the new procedure is applicable in a wide variety of cases, and if it offers significant benefits not available by using the old procedures, then it might be best for each physician to learn enough about the new diagnostic procedure to make some of its benefits available to all patients without referral. Patients requiring further tests would be referred to specialists.

The second approach is more likely to serve the patients' basic needs without referral and is therefore more convenient for the patients. The first approach is more likely to appeal to those physicians who would prefer not to learn the new procedure. Whose convenience is more important: that of the physicians who would rather not go to the trouble of learning the new diagnostic procedure or that of the patients who would rather not pay and then wait for referrals?

Returning to the question of whether teachers should be required to use calculators and computers regularly in all mathematics classes, similarities should be apparent between the issue facing the group of physicians and the issue facing the faculty of the elementary school. In both cases, a new service must be delivered to a wide variety of clients. In both cases, disagreement arises over who should provide the service: all professionals or only certain experts. In both cases, the degree to which the burden of change should be shared by the professionals and the clients causes tension.

A few important differences also exist. First, with few exceptions, students cannot change teachers. In particular, elementary school students do not normally have access to educational opportunities other than those offered through their local school districts; they are a captive audience. This places additional burdens of responsibility on school districts. By contrast, changing physicians is relatively easy. Second, most elementary schools have no computer expert to whom students can be referred on a regular basis. Even if such a resource person were available at school, delays involved in referrals of hundreds of students could probably not be tolerated. Given these constraints, the only responsible answer to the question of whether teachers should be required to use calculators and computers regularly is affirmative. For millions of elementary school children, the issue comes down to this: If their classroom teacher does not show them how to use calculators and computers in mathematics, nobody will. They have no other way to learn how.

CONCEPT DEVELOPMENT AND THE NEW TECHNOLOGIES

From kindergarten to graduate school, concept development and problem-solving give mathematics its meaning and relevance. These aspects of mathematics must also be the focus of the school mathematics curriculum. Fortunately, the new technologies offer significant opportunities to teach concepts and problem-solving in ways that empower students and motivate them to continue their study of mathematics.

Concept development in elementary school mathematics should rely heavily on the use of concrete materials that give the student the opportunity to focus on the features of geometrical objects and the transformations described in various processes. The following examples illustrate the use of the computer as an extension of concrete operations and as a thinking environment.

Example 1: Investigating Volume with Manipulatives and Computer Simulation*

Literally millions of students have used LOGO to explore plane geometry, create graphic designs, and just doodle. A smaller number of students and teachers have used LOGO to develop microworlds that model concepts or processes found in the natural world or in the study of mathematics.

This example presents an interactive microworld that aids the development of the concept of volume. Specifically, students are asked to determine the volume of the largest open-top box that can be created from a rectangular piece of paper by clipping out square corners and folding up the sides. Gill (1984) and Channell (1984) addressed this topic by using concrete materials and a computer program written in BASIC. This example builds on their insights by using LogoWriter to

*Used by permission from *The Computing Teacher* (February 1988). Published by the International Council for Computers in Education.

create a highly interactive and information-rich microworld. In the true spirit of LOGO, this microworld is easy to get into, and the possibilities are hard to exhaust.

All the programming presented in this example is written in LogoWriter, published by LOGO Computer Systems, Inc. and requires a LogoWriter language disk to operate. This version of LOGO offers several enhancements over previous versions, including the mixing of graphics and textual material on the screen, a FILL command, and several convenient I/O (input/output) features. The programming used to create the microworld is identical in the Apple and IBM versions of LogoWriter.

A Concrete Approach

The learning theories of Piaget and Van Hiele both assert that school mathematics should introduce new concepts through the use of manipulative materials. Computer simulations should be viewed as a rich extension of experiences with manipulative materials, not as a substitute for the "real thing." For children, a direct, hands-on approach to this problem has great appeal. Figure 6.1 illustrates the process described in the list that follows.

FIGURE 6.1   Graph Paper Boxes

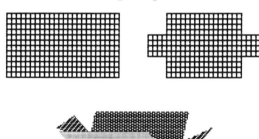

Step 1. Obtain a piece of grid paper cut to the specified dimensions.

Step 2. Decide on the length of the corner cuts to be made.

Step 3. Cut the corner squares out and discard.

Step 4. Fold up the sides and apply tape at the corners.

Step 5. Fill the interior with unit cubes.

In trying out this activity with fourth-graders, 1-cm cubes and grid paper with 1-cm squares were used. By counting the cubes necessary to fill the box, the students easily determined the box's volume.

If a class works in small groups, answers and procedures can be compared in a teacher-led discussion in which each group reports the dimensions of its corner cuts and the volume of the resulting box. These data should be entered into a table on the chalkboard by the teacher (see Figure 6.2).

One of the features of a tabular display of this nature is that missing values are easily identified. For instance, if your students are working with a 14-by-14 grid, there are six possible boxes that can be constructed by using the procedures outlined above. If your class is divided into five groups, at least one of the six possible boxes will not be built. Missing data of this nature can be quickly identified when

FIGURE 6.2   **Sugar Cube Bar Graph**

GRID SIZE = 7 X 7

#	Volume
1	25
2	18
3	3

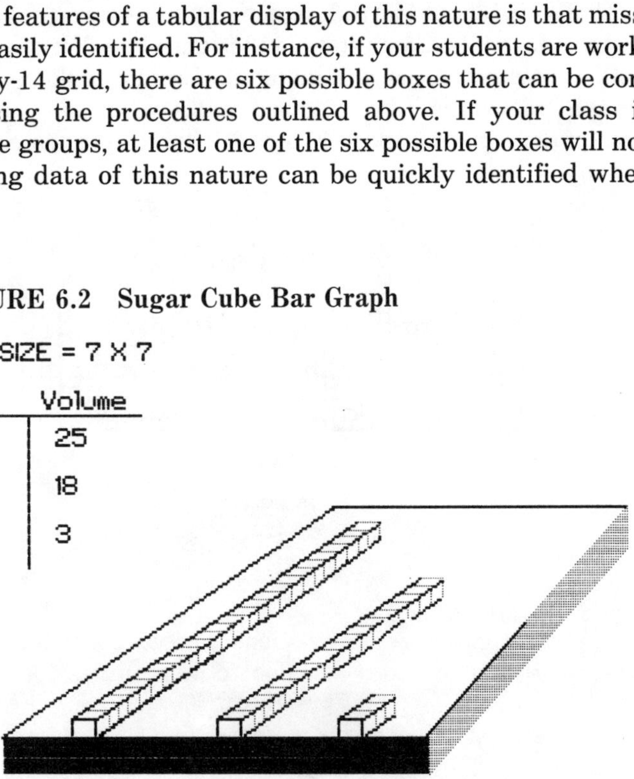

using a table to summarize class findings. The remaining boxes can then be constructed and the data entered into the table.

Once the table is complete, the data can be represented as a graph by arranging the cubes from each box in columns laid out on a desk top. The columns should be arranged in the same order as their respective entries in the table, from smallest corner cut to largest corner cut. This creates a concrete model of a bar graph. Figure 6.2 illustrates the table and three-dimensional display obtained using a 7-by-7 grid. Children can use the columns of cubes as guides while drawing two-dimensional graphs on paper by tracing around each column and marking the position of each cube.

Higher-Order Questions

Once the table, display, and graphs are complete, a number of higher-order questions should be considered.

1. Why must the corner cuts be square?

2. What is the relationship between the size of the corner cut and the height of the box?

3. In comparing two boxes, will the taller box always have the greater volume?

4. For a square starting grid with fixed dimensions, what happens to the volume of the boxes as the size of the corner cuts increases?

5. Does the answer to Question 4 depend on the size of the original grid? Repeat the experiment using a 9-by-9 starting grid, a 12-by-12 starting grid, and so on.

6. Does the answer to Question 4 depend on the shape of the starting grid? Try starting with a rectangular grid (say, 7-by-9) rather than a square grid (7-by-7).

Investigating these questions involves students in problem-solving activities and provides excellent opportunities for group discussion. Some students should be encouraged to start with various sizes of square grids. Others might want to start with rectangular grids rather than square ones.

Significance of the Chart and Bar Graph

One observation likely to arise from a study of the data concerns the curve formed by connecting the tops of the bars of the bar graph. Obviously the choice of corner cut affects the volume of the box. Furthermore, a maximum volume is clearly visible in both the table and the graphs. This notion of a local maximum is important in itself and deserves attention and discussion. Another question might be explored: Could an even greater maximum volume be found by using decimal corner cuts (such as 2.5 units on a side)?

Decimal corner cuts lead to decimal volumes, which are not easily counted when using concrete materials. However, if students have understood the activities up to this point, a shift to another approach is both appropriate and effective.

From Concrete to Semiconcrete Simulation

The advantage in extending the lesson with a computer simulation is that the problem can be examined more quickly and in greater depth. This is particularly true in the case of decimal corner cuts.

The LogoWriter procedures in Listing 6.1 simulate the activities discussed above. Starting the simulation is easy once the procedures are typed into a LogoWriter file. After loading the file, type START in response to the flashing cursor and hit RETURN.

In a few moments, the following prompt and information will appear at the bottom of the sceen:

```
[ENTER THE GRID SIZE]
[SMALLEST:  3 BY 3   LARGEST: 14 BY 14]
[EXAMPLE: 10 BY 12]
```

This is where students select the dimensions of their grid. The starting grid must be rectangular (squares included), each side having a length between 3 and 14 units inclusive. Enter the choices for width and length, using the format indicated in the prompt: two whole numbers separated by spaces and the word BY. The first number will become the width of the grid and the second number its length. Then hit RETURN. In response to the entry, LogoWriter draws the grid and a pair of coordinate axes, which will be used for a bar graph.

When these graphics have been completed, another prompt will appear asking students to ENTER SIDE OF SQUARE CORNER NIBBLE. This is their chance to specify the length of the side of the corner cut, or NIBBLE as it is called in this program. For example, if students want to nibble out a 2-by-2 corner cut, they enter the number 2, then hit RETURN.

LISTING 6.1   Computer Box Simulation

```
TO START
RG CC RECYCLE
SHOW [ENTER THE GRID SIZE]
SHOW [SMALLEST: 3 BY 3 LARGEST: 14 BY 14]
SHOW [EXAMPLE: 10 BY 12]
MAKE "SIZE READLISTCC
MAKE "H FIRST :SIZE
MAKE "V LAST :SIZE
IFELSE (:H < :V) [MAKE "NB :H MAKE "Z :V] [MAKE "NB :V MAKE "Z :H]
HT HLABEL GETON
END


TO HLABEL
PU
SETPOS SE 20 -10 PD LABEL [#1 2 3 4 5 6] PU
SETPOS SE 10 45 PD LABEL "V PU
SETPOS SE 10 35 PD LABEL "O PU
SETPOS SE 10 25 PD LABEL "L PU
SETPOS SE 80 -30 PD LABEL [V#1 =] PU
SETPOS SE 80 -40 PD LABEL [V#2 =] PU
SETPOS SE 80 -50 PD LABEL [V#3 =] PU
SETPOS SE 80 -60 PD LABEL [V#4 =] PU
SETPOS SE 80 -70 PD LABEL [V#5 =] PU
SETPOS SE 80 -80 PD LABEL [V#6 =] PU
END


TO GETON
GRID
TYPE [ENTER SIDE OF CORNER NIBBLE ]
MAKE "N FIRST READLISTCC
IF :N > :NB/2 [GETON]
IF :N < 0 [GETON]
IF (MEMBER? :N [0 1 2 3 4 5 6]) [NIBBLE]
SOLID GRAPH
TYPE [ANOTHER FIGURE? (Y/N/STOP) ]
MAKE "ANS FIRST READLISTCC
IF :ANS = "N [START]
IF :ANS = "STOP [STOPALL]
ADDON
END


TO GRID
HT PU
SETPOS SE -130 90 SETH 90
REPEAT (:V)[PD FD :H*8 BK :H*8 PU RT 90 FD 8 LT 90]
PD FD :H*8 BK :H*8 LT 90
REPEAT (:H)[PD FD :V*8 BK :V*8 PU RT 90 FD 8 LT 90]
PD FD :V*8 BK :V*8 PU
SETPOS SE 15 0 SETH 0 PD
FD 80 BK 80 RT 90 REPEAT 7 [FD 15 RT 90 FD 3 BK 3 LT 90] PU
END
```

Cont'd

LISTING 6-1   Cont'd

```
TO NIBBLE
PU SETPOS SE -130 90 SETH 90 BLANK
PU SETPOS SE (-130+:H*8) 90 SETH 180 BLANK
PU SETPOS SE (-130+:H*8) (90-:V*8) SETH 270 BLANK
PU SETPOS SE -130 (90-:V*8) SETH 0 BLANK
END


TO BLANK
FD 5
REPEAT (:N)[RT 90 FD 5 REPEAT (:N)[PD FILL PU FD 8] BK (:N*8+5) LT 90 FD 8]
END


TO SOLID
MAKE "MH (:H - :N*2)
MAKE "MV (:V - :N*2)
PU SETPOS SE (-130+:N*8) -89 SETH 0 PD
BOX
END


TO BOX
REPEAT 2[FD :N*8 RT 90 FD :MH*8 RT 90]
FD :N*8
SETH 70 FD :MV*8
SETH 90 FD :MH*8
RT 90 FD :N*8
SETH 250 FD :MV*8
SETH 0 FD :N*8
SETH 70 FD :MV*8
PU
END


TO GRAPH
PU SETPOS SE 15 0 SETH 90
MAKE "VOL (:MV*:MH*:N)
PD FD :N*15 LT 90 FD :VOL/3+1
IFELSE (MEMBER? :N [1 2 3 4 5 6]) [PU SETPOS SE 115 (-10*:N-20) PD LABEL :VOL]
[SHOW [THE VOLUME IS ] SHOW :VOL SHOW [HIT THE SPACE BAR] MAKE "D READCHAR ]
PU SETPOS SE 15 0
END


TO ADDON
UNSOLID
IF (MEMBER? :N [0 1 2 3 4 5 6]) [ZAP]
GETON
END


TO UNSOLID
PU SETPOS SE (-130+:N*8) -89 SETH 0
PD PE BOX
END


TO ZAP
PU SETPOS SE -130 90
SETH 90 PD PE
REPEAT ((:Z+1)*4)[FD :Z*8 RT 90 FD 1 RT 90 FD :Z*8 LT 90 FD 1 LT 90]
PU HOME
END
```

160

Results

Figure 6.3 shows the result of the following series of prompts and responses:

```
[ENTER THE GRID SIZE]
[SMALLEST:  3 BY 3   LARGEST: 14 BY 14]
[EXAMPLE: 10 BY 12]
11 BY 11
ENTER SIDE OF SQUARE CORNER NIBBLE 1
```

LogoWriter responds by shading the corner cuts on the grid, drawing the box, calculating the volume, and plotting a bar graph of the volume. The volume of the box is reported as V#1 = 81. (The notation V#5 is used to identify the volume of a box with a 5-by-5 corner cut, and so forth. Notice that no units are printed. The program leaves it to the instructor to reinforce the concept of units of volume.

Following this activity, students will be asked to respond to another prompt at the bottom of the screen. The prompt asks, ADD ANOTHER FIGURE'S VOLUME? (Y/N/STOP).

If students take the Y option, a new grid of the same size will appear on the screen, and they will see the prompt ENTER SIDE OF SQUARE CORNER NIBBLE. A box of the appropriate dimensions will be drawn and its volume entered in the table and bar graph. This

FIGURE 6.3   Integer Corner Cut

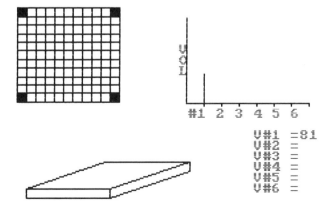

procedure may be repeated until students have determined the volume of every possible box created from the starting grid when using whole-number corner nibbles. If they enter a corner cut which is too large for the starting grid, the entry is rejected and the prompt reappears. They then have the option to enter a new number or a number previously accepted by the program.

If students respond with an N, all information is erased from the screen and the program starts over. They must take this option if they wish to change the size of the grid.

The STOP option is provided for those who want a printout of the screen graphics before moving on to another grid size. When the flashing cursor appears at the bottom of the screen, move it down to a new line and type PRINTSCREEN. If the printer is on and the paper correctly in place, LogoWriter will print out the grid, box, graph, and table as they appear on the screen. It will not print out the record of prompts and responses at the bottom of the screen; if students want to review those, scroll through them by using the cursor controls, taking notes as desired.

Decimal Corner Cuts

Decimal corner cuts enable students to extend the search for the box of largest volume that can be obtained from their starting grid. To try a decimal corner cut, enter a decimal number at the prompt ENTER SIZE OF SQUARE CORNER NIBBLE. The grid will not shade the corner cut, but the box will be drawn and the bar graph plotted. The numerical answer will appear at the bottom of the screen and should be written down. For example, Figure 6.4 shows the graphics screen output for a decimal corner cut of 1.8 units on an 11-by-11 starting grid. The volume is displayed at the bottom of the screen as follows:

```
[THE VOLUME IS]
98.568
[HIT THE SPACE BAR]
```

When the space bar is touched, the box is erased, leaving the un-used grid, graph, and table of data. LogoWriter then prompts for the next corner nibble. By repeating this procedure several times over an

FIGURE 6.4   Decimal Corner Cut

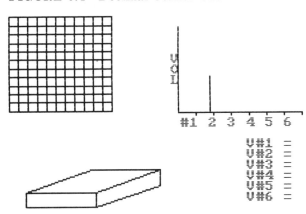

interval (for instance, from 2.0 to 3.0 in increments of .1), a more complete graph can be obtained.

Conclusion

In this example, LogoWriter was used to create a computer-based microworld. This microworld was created as an extension of an investigation of volume that began with the use of concrete manipulatives. This approach guarantees that the minds of students have a clear link between the objects and activities depicted on the computer screen and the mathematical concepts and processes encountered in using concrete manipulatives. The purpose of the computer simulation is to speed up the examination of many different boxes and to represent the data gathered in tabular, graphic, and algebraic form. The power of the computer enables students to do these tasks quickly and accurately, thereby freeing them to focus on the mathematical concepts themselves, rather than on computational tasks, and to look for patterns in the collected data.

Students using the microworld presented in this example have a great deal of freedom to experiment. Printouts of the screen images may be posted on a bulletin board with other results. Higher-order questions may be posed and posted for study along with the graphics. In short, given a reasonable length of time and a nonthreatening, inquisitive atmosphere, the opportunity exists for the development of many mathematical insights. This type of dialogue encourages good mathematics and invites full participation on the part of the learner.

Example 2. Exploring Fractal Geometry Using LOGO*

One manifestation of a new and refreshing interest in geometry these days is a reevaluation of what we mean by geometry and what students ought to know about the subject. From all appearances, this reevaluation will prescribe a much broader experience, including work in transformational, non-Euclidean, and other geometries. This example presents a method for introducing students to fractal geometry using LOGO, a geometrical thinking environment familiar to millions of elementary and secondary school students.

Dimensionality in Euclidean Geometry

Traditional mathematics asserts that the universe is made up only of one-, two-, and three-dimensional objects. Students are often introduced to this notion of dimensionality as follows:

1. A point has no dimension.
2. Move a point a given distance in one direction and you sweep out a one-dimensional line segment.
3. Move every point on a line segment in a single direction perpendicular to the segment and you sweep out a portion of a two-dimensional plane, such as a square.
4. Move every point on a square in a single direction perpendicular to the square and you sweep out a three-dimensional space, such as that occupied by a cube.

A direct application of this approach to dimensionality is shown in Figure 6.5. In the first row of the figure, three line segments are drawn. Each segment has been divided into two, three, or four parts

---

*Used by permission of the *Journal of Computers in Mathematics and Science Teaching*, P.O. Box 2966, Charlottesville, VA 22902.

FIGURE 6.5   One, Two, and Three Dimensions

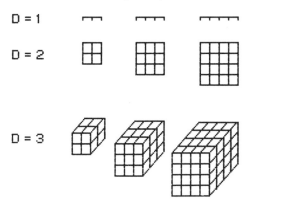

(P). As these three original segments are used to generate squares and cubes, the number (N) of smaller squares and cubes produced depends on the division of each original line segment according to the following relationship:

$$N = P^D$$

where P = number of parts in the original line segment,

N = number of parts in the square or cube created,

D = the dimension of the created object.

For example, the line segment divided into two parts generates a three-dimensional cube having $2^3 = 8$ smaller cubic sections. The line segment divided into three parts generates a two-dimensional square having $3^2 = 9$ smaller square sections.

The expression $N = P^D$ may be rewritten using logarithms as

$$D = \frac{\log(N)}{\log(P)}$$

Using this expression, you may compute the dimension of the object in the lower right-hand corner of Figure 6.5. The number (N) of parts generated is 64. The number of parts (P) in the original line segment used to generate the object is 4.

$$D = \frac{\log(64)}{\log(4)} = 3$$

The limitations of this approach to dimensionality are obvious once you address them. For example, lines drawn by children scribbling on a sheet of paper may be one-dimensional, but the space filled by such exuberant doodles begins to take on some of the qualities of a two-dimensional plane as the children continue to go over and over the page with their pencils or crayons. Similarly, a piece of two-dimensional paper smashed into a dense wad begins to take on the appearance of a three-dimensional object. Euclidean geometry is of little use in describing such ragged, crumpled shapes.

If one-, two-, and three-dimensional models are too limited to describe certain objects, what is needed? The answer is objects with fractional dimensions and a geometry that has a way to characterize roughness, such as fractal geometry.

A New Dimensionality

The first new concept that fractal geometry offers is that of fractional (or "fractal") dimensions. In this geometry, objects can have unfamiliar dimensions: 0.8; 1.26; 2.4; and so on. Where do such numbers come from? To answer that question, it will help to make an observation regarding the kinds of objects counted when determining the values of P and N in the expression $D = \log(N)/\log(P)$. In the examples already worked, line segments were counted to determine the value of P, and squares or cubes were counted to obtain the number N. In fractal geometry, it is common to count only lines for the values of both P and N.

To illustrate this point, consider Figures 6.6–6.9*. This sequence of figures shows the first four steps in the creation of a Koch snowflake curve, which has a fractal dimension of approximately 1.26. Computing this value is relatively easy. Begin by focusing your attention on one side of the triangle in Figure 6.6. Imagine the side divided into thirds (i.e., $P = 3$). This three-part segment is called the initiator segment for the fractal. Now examine Figure 6.7. Notice that each of the

---

*Figures 6.6–6.26 were created using a LOGO procedure. The names of the procedure is DO. This procedure takes one input—for example, DO 0 or DO 1. The captions for the figures represent the command used to create them.

FIGURE 6.6   Snowflake: DO 0

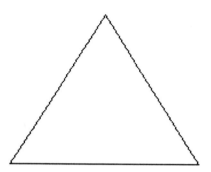

three sides of Figure 6.6 has been replaced by a sequence of four segments ($N = 4$), each of which has the same length as the three parts
of the initiator segment. This sequence of four segments is called the
generator of the fractal. Continuing your examination, look at Figure
6.8. The same process has been repeated on a smaller scale, replacing
every segment in Figure 6.7 with a new sequence of four segments. At
each level of this process, a segment of length 3 is replaced by a sequence of segments of length 4. The process can be repeated more
times (see Figure 6.9).

FIGURE 6.7   Snowflake: DO 1

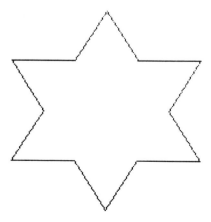

FIGURE 6.8   Snowflake: DO 2

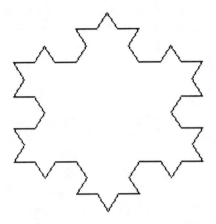

Substituting these values in the expression

$$D = \frac{\log(N)}{\log(P)}$$

yields

$$D = \frac{\log(4)}{\log(3)} = 1.261859507$$

FIGURE 6.9   Snowflake: DO 3

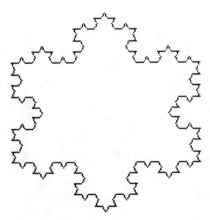

Thus, fractal dimension is a measure of the relative complexities of the initiator and generator segments of a fractal. The more complex the generator in relation to the initiator, the greater the fractal dimension of the object. This concept of fractal dimension provides us with a measure of the "roughness" of an object. For instance, a thoroughly crumpled line might have a fractal dimension of 2.4. This happens to be the fractal dimension of two complex but very different objects: a human hemoglobin molecule and a tightly wadded piece of paper. A less crumpled curve is shown in the sequence of objects illustrated in Figures 6.10–6.13. The curve approximated by these figures has a fractal dimension of 1.5.

An interesting possibility occurs as soon as the fractal dimension of an object reaches 2. Some such objects are capable of completely covering a section of a plane, even if the object doing the covering is a line! Such lines are called plane-filling curves and are the ultimate expression of the word "scribble." The sequence of objects illustrated in Figures 6.14–6.17 represents the development of such a plane-filling curve.

Finally, what about objects with fractal dimension between 0 and 1? A figure with a fractal dimension of 0.8 would fail to "connect" its points into a line. Such figures are often called "dust," because they consist of unconnected points.

Self-Similarity

The second important concept that fractal geometry offers is that of "self-similarity." This attribute may be described as the repetition of some geometrical theme on different scales: Little pieces of the object

FIGURE 6.10   Dragon Curve: DO 0

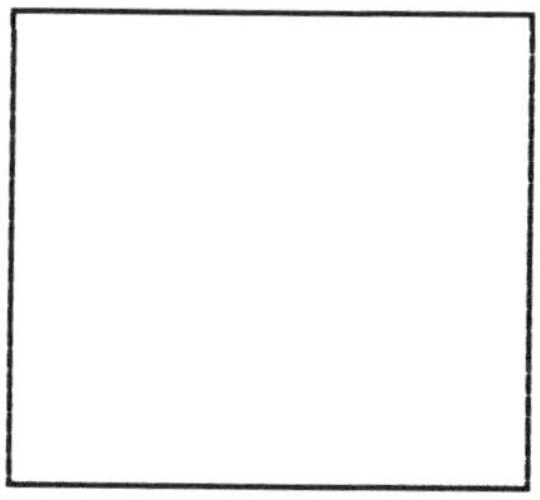

FIGURE 6.11 Dragon Curve: DO 1

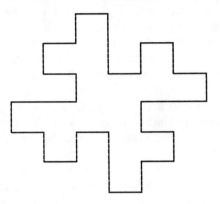

or shape look like larger pieces. This quality is found in all of the fractals discussed in this example.

The most basic expression of the repeated geometrical theme of a fractal is the fractal's generator segment. (The generator segments for the figures are found in Table 6.1.) Once the generator segment has been defined for a given starting polygon, the modification is applied to all the sides of the polygon. In the case of the Koch curve, the effect of this first transformation is shown in Figure 6.7. The next step is to

FIGURE 6.12 Dragon Curve: DO 2

FIGURE 6.13   Dragon Curve: DO 3

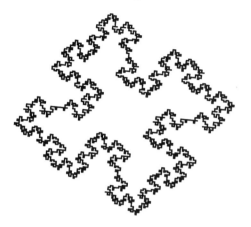

FIGURE 6.14   Plane-Filling Curve: DO 0

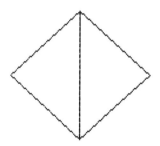

FIGURE 6.15   Plane-Filling Curve: DO 1

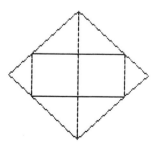

FIGURE 6.16   Plane-Filling Curve: DO 2

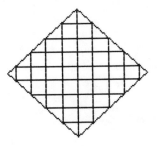

repeat the process again, dividing each side of the polygon shown in Figure 6.7 into thirds and inserting a triangular bulge in the middle. This produces Figure 6.8. Repeating the process results in Figure 6.9. Taken as a whole, this process produces bulges on bulges on bulges, and so on. This is the scaling phenomenon: the repetition of the same theme on different scales.

An interesting variation on this theme is to turn the bulges inward rather than outward. The sequence of objects generated using this approach appears in Figures 6.18–6.21. By changing the shape of the generator segment, interesting variations can be obtained in the final form of the fractal. For example, Figures 6.22–6.26 show the development of a flower-like object from an equilateral triangle. The differences between the Koch snowflake curve and this flower-like object arise from the differences in their generator segments.

FIGURE 6.17   Plane-Filling Curve: DO 3

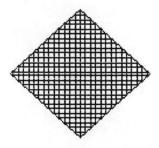

Table 6.1   Generator Segments

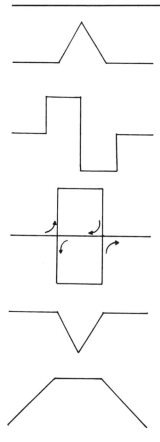

Home-Grown Fractals

Producing fractals on a school or home computer is relatively easy, providing students have a copy of the LOGO language. Fortunately, no special version of LOGO is needed to write procedures that generate fractals. Although LogoWriter was used to write the procedures for this example, any version of LOGO would have the necessary features. For example, consider the program listing (Listing 6.2) for the set of procedures called FLAKE. The main procedure is TO DO :N. In using this program, the user types in the command DO 0 or DO 1 or DO 2,

FIGURE 6.18   Inverted Snowflake: DO 0

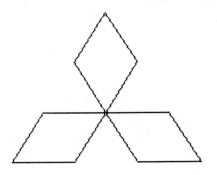

FIGURE 6.19   Inverted Snowflake: DO 1

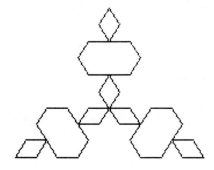

FIGURE 6.20   Inverted Snowflake: DO 2

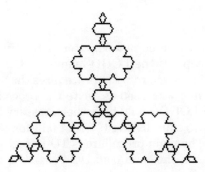

FIGURE 6.21 Inverted Snowflake: DO 3

FIGURE 6.22 Flower: DO 0

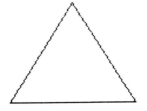

FIGURE 6.23 Flower: DO 1

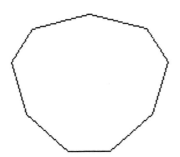

FIGURE 6.24   Flower: DO 2

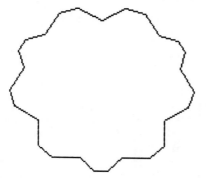

FIGURE 6.25   Flower: DO 3

FIGURE 6.26   Flower: DO 4

176

LISTING 6.2   FLAKE

```
TO DO :N
START :N
REPEAT 3 [ LINE :L RT 120 ]
END

TO START :N
MAKE "X 1
REPEAT :N [ MAKE "X 3*:X ]
MAKE "L 162/:X
CT RG PU HT RT 60 BK 90 LT 30 PD
END

TO LINE :L
IF :N = 0 [FD :L]
IF :N = 1 [MOVE1 :L]
IF :N = 2 [MOVE2 :L]
IF :N = 3 [MOVE3 :L]
IF :N = 4 [MOVE4 :L]
END

TO MOVE1 :L
FD :L LT 60 FD :L RT 120
FD :L LT 60 FD :L
END

TO MOVE2 :L
MOVE1 :L LT 60 MOVE1 :L RT 120
MOVE1 :L LT 60 MOVE1 :L
END

TO MOVE3 :L
MOVE2 :L LT 60 MOVE2 :L RT 120
MOVE2 :L LT 60 MOVE2 :L
END

TO MOVE4 :L
MOVE3 :L LT 60 MOVE3 :L RT 120
MOVE3 :L LT 60 MOVE3 :L
END
```

and so forth. In the case of the command DO 0, Figure 6.6 is generated. The command DO 1 produces Figure 6.7. DO 2 results in Figure 6.8, and so on.

In each case, the START :N procedure is called immediately. This procedure identifies the number of parts into which the initiator segment is to be divided. In the case of FLAKE, the initiator segment is divided into three equal parts. This is defined in the expression RE-PEAT :N[MAKE "X 3*:X]. If a four-part division is needed, the user must modify the line to read REPEAT :N[MAKE "X 4*:X].

The next line, MAKE "L 162/:X, determines the size of the original polygon and the segment lengths at various levels of roughness. Using an IBM compatible computer, the number 162 produces a large starting triangle (DO 0 level). Users should experiment with this number to determine the best value for various starting polygons.

The line CT RG PU HT RT 60 BK 90 LT 30 PD merely positions one corner of the equilateral triangle in the lower left-hand corner of the screen. Once again, individual users should experiment with commands to center the original polygon in the display.

Once START is complete, the DO :N procedure executes the command REPEAT 3[LINE :L RT 120]. This command establishes the original polygon as an equilateral triangle: a three-sided polygon with exterior angles of 120 degrees. If students want to start with a square, use REPEAT 4[LINE :L 90], and so on.

The LINE :L procedure essentially defines the level of roughness desired in the object. A level 0 roughness has no bulges. A level 1 roughness has a bulge on each side of the original triangle. A level 2 roughness has "bulges on the bulges" roughness. A level 3 roughness has "bulges on the bulges on the bulges" roughness.

The procedure MOVE1 :L describes how to make the generator segment for the fractal. At this point in the program, students have the most freedom to experiment. Every new generator will produce a new fractal. Notice that, like the fractal images generated, the procedures MOVE2 :L, MOVE3 :L, and MOVE4 :L have the same form as the generator procedure, MOVE1 :L. Once the generator procedure MOVE1 :L has been written, all the other MOVE procedures should have the same structure, differing only in the numbers built into the MOVE procedure names.

Experienced LOGO programmers will find FLAKE a clumsy use of the LOGO language, but FLAKE was written just to show the similarity in structure of a fractal and its source code. A more streamlined set of codes is provided in FLAKE2 (Listing 6.3). For the novice LOGO programmer, FLAKE2 reveals less than FLAKE about the process of creating fractals, but it also offers more levels of "roughness" to the user, as well as an elegant use of the recursive features of the LOGO language.

Playing with Plane-Filling Curves

The set of procedures named PLANE (Listing 6.4) may be used to investigate the concept of a plane-filling curve. The curve used to gener-

LISTING 6.3   FLAKE 2

```
TO DO :N
START
REPEAT 3 [IFELSE :N = 0
[FD :L] [LINE :N] RT 120]
END

TO START
MAKE "X 1
REPEAT :N [MAKE "X 3*:X]
MAKE "L 162/:X
CT RG PU HT RT 60 BK 90
LT 30 PD
END

TO LINE :Y
IFELSE :Y = 1 [FD :L LT 60
FD :L RT 120 FD :L LT 60
FD :L] [LINE :Y-1 LT 60
LINE :Y-1 RT 120 LINE :Y-1
LT 60 LINE :Y-1]
END
```

ate Figures 6.14–6.17 is called a Peano curve, in honor of the mathematician G. Peano. Other well-known plane-filling curves were developed by D. Hilbert and W. Sierpinski. Naturally, no computer program is capable of tracing such a curve. The infinite number of points involved could never be calculated, much less plotted. Nevertheless, the theoretical process of defining such a plane-filling curve can be investigated with a computer. If students experiment with the plane-filling curve presented in this example, they will discover that the object on their computer screen appears to be filled completely by using four or five levels of roughness. The difference between this apparent success and the actual mathematical situation should be explained to the uninitiated.

Student Creativity

Let students try a variety of starting polygons. Take triangular and square spirals and fractalize them. Invent complicated generators that wander off the initiator segment in tortured paths. In the process, ponder the attributes of the figures generated. For example, Figures 6.10–6.13 all have the same area. Why? Do any of the other figures have this attribute? Do some figures approach some area as a limit? What about their perimeters?

LISTING 6.4   PLANE

```
TO DO :N
START
LINE :L
END

TO START
MAKE "X 1
REPEAT :N[MAKE "X 3*:X]
MAKE "L 120/:X
CT PU HOME HT BK 60 PD
END

TO LINE :L
IF :N = 0 [LT 45 REPEAT
4[FD :L*.707 RT 90]
RT 45 FD :L]
IF :N = 1 [MOVE1 :L]
IF :N = 2 [MOVE2 :L]
IF :N = 3 [MOVE3 :L]
IF :N = 4 [MOVE4 :L]
END

TO MOVE1 :L
FD :L LT 90 FD :L RT 90
FD :L RT 90 FD :L RT 90
FD :L LT 90 FD :L LT 90
FD :L LT 90 FD :L RT 90
FD :L
END

TO MOVE2 :L
MOVE1 :L LT 90 MOVE1 :L RT 90
MOVE1 :L RT 90 MOVE1 :L RT 90
MOVE1 :L LT 90 MOVE1 :L LT 90
MOVE1 :L LT 90 MOVE1 :L RT 90
MOVE1 :L
END

TO MOVE3 :L
MOVE2 :L LT 90 MOVE2 :L RT 90
MOVE2 :L RT 90 MOVE2 :L RT 90
MOVE2 :L LT 90 MOVE2 :L LT 90
MOVE2 :L LT 90 MOVE2 :L RT 90
MOVE2 :L
END

TO MOVE4 :L
MOVE3 :L LT 90 MOVE3 :L RT 90
MOVE3 :L RT 90 MOVE3 :L RT 90
MOVE3 :L LT 90 MOVE3 :L LT 90
MOVE3 :L LT 90 MOVE3 :L RT 90
MOVE3 :L
END
```

Fractal geometry offers students the opportunity to explore a new field of mathematics by using a new technology. Here indeed is a new opportunity for students to use their imaginations and their powers of observation and deduction.

Example 3: Exploring Geometry Using Geometric Supposer

Although LOGO is the preferred mathematical computer language for elementary school children, other excellent programs can encourage the exploration of geometry. One of the best programs available is the Geometric Supposer series, published by Sunburst Communications. This series of programs comes in four parts: Points and Lines, Triangles, Circles, and Quadrilaterals.

The Supposer programs offer students a friendly environment in which to investigate the properties of geometric objects. They also offer the teacher well-developed lesson plans and activity sheets. For example, pages T3 and T4 of the teacher notes for the Triangles program are reproduced as Figure 6.27. In this activity, students are given a series of tasks that will reveal the relationship among the three interior angles and one exterior angle of a triangle. The goal is for students to discover in the data collected a pattern that will support a conjecture or set of conjectures about the angles. The student pages appear on the left side of the figure in small print and the anticipated conjectures appear on the right side.

Each Supposer program comes with a complete set of teacher notes and student worksheets. These materials are ready to use and provide an excellent basis for independent work or group discussion. The manner in which students gather their data makes the activities practical.

Getting Started

When the computer program is started, the screen is divided into three windows (see Figure 6.28). The right side of the screen displays a graphics work area called the construction pad, where objects may be drawn and labeled. A data area where measurements may be recorded is located on the left side of the screen, and a window for menus and prompts is at the bottom.

The user draws, labels, and measures objects by selecting options

FIGURE 6.27 Geometric Supposer Teacher Notes

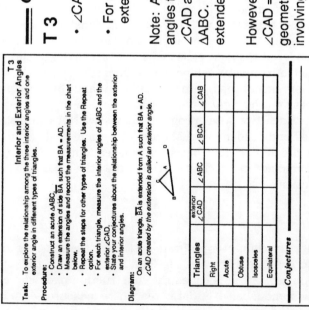

=== *Conjectures* ===

T 3

- $\angle CAD = \angle ACB + \angle CBA$

- For acute triangles only, the measure of each exterior angle is greater than any interior angle.

Note: Actually, for any $\triangle ABC$, there are two exterior angles for each angle in the triangle. For example, $\angle CAD$ and $\angle BAE$ are both exterior angles for $\angle A$ in $\triangle ABC$. $\overline{BA}$ is extended to create $\angle CAD$; $\overline{CA}$ is extended to create $\angle BAE$.

However, since $\angle CAD$ and $\angle BAE$ are vertical angles, $\angle CAD = \angle BAE$. In this problem, and most others in geometry, we are interested only in the relationships involving <u>one</u> exterior angle at each vertex.

182

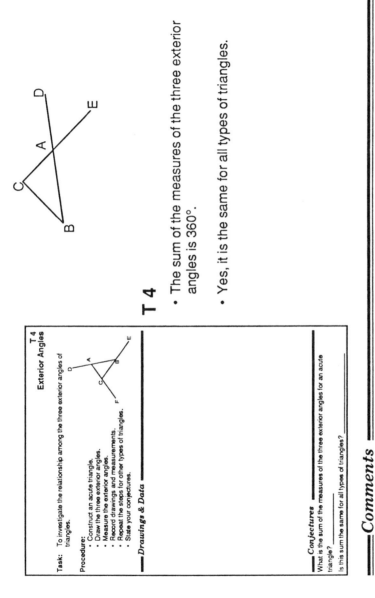

T 4

- The sum of the measures of the three exterior angles is 360°.

- Yes, it is the same for all types of triangles.

Comments

Reprinted from *Geometric Supposer Teacher Notes*, with permission of Sunburst Communications.

FIGURE 6.28   Geometric Supposer Screen

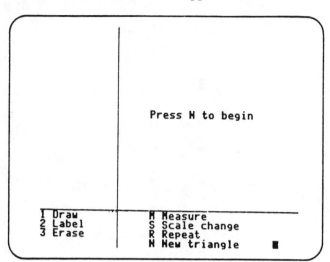

Used with permission of Sunburst Communications.

from the window at the bottom of the screen. Learning what can be done with the Supposer is as simple as scanning the options found in the various menus. As a result, complete novices can sit down and learn the basics in a matter of minutes.

Once a figure has been drawn, a number of measurement tools are available. For example, users may measure length, perimeter, area, angle, and circumference easily and quickly. As each measurement is made, it is recorded in the data window. Students then transfer these data to their activity sheets. Using this approach, students can quickly examine a number of figures for certain properties, logging their data and sketching their figures as they go. As data are gathered, patterns emerge and lead to the statement of conjectures: educated guesses in the form of generalizations such as, "For all triangles, the exterior angle is equal to the sum of the measures of the two remote interior angles."

A Friendly Geometry

Discoveries such as this are easily within the reach of middle school and junior high students. Notice that no attempt is made to prove the conjecture. The goal is concept development. The approach is inductive mathematics, and the geometry is friendly. One frequent byproduct is a great deal of enthusiasm for doing geometry with the Supposer. Students who leave junior high already knowing and understanding many of the theorems taught in high school geometry will enter that course with a great advantage over students who have never explored geometry informally.

Example 4: Investigating Tessellations Using a Computer Graphics Package

The dedicated doodler delights in the exploration of line, shape, and form. Some doodlers create complex, carefully detailed images on their faculty meeting agendas. Others explore the elegant, cleverly-crafted logo, caricature, or tessellation. Like mathematical theorems, such designs emphasize clarity and conciseness.

Tessellations appeal strongly, both as mathematical objects and as art objects. For instance, a number of important geometrical concepts may be illustrated in the context of a discussion of tessellations: tilings, translation, reflection, rotation, symmetry, and so on. Tessellations can also be reminiscent of something beyond mathematics. For example, Escher's drawings may appeal because the tilings are birds and fish and a host of other objects that seem totally unrelated to mathematics. His unexpected joining of art and mathematics amazes students and challenges the imagination.

In creating Escher-type designs, both mathematical and artistic concerns must be taken into account. Here is a grand opportunity for cross-pollination between mathematics and art. Here also is an opportunity to challenge both the left and right hemispheres of the brain, for both skill (left hemisphere) and insight (right hemisphere) are required to design a tessellation that suggests some familiar object or living creature.

This example deals with the search for such images and is dedicated to readers who remember with happiness the embedded-figures worksheets we did as children, which began, "In this line drawing there are hidden objects. See if you can find three dogs, a camel, two balls. . . ."

Reprinted by permission of *The Virginia Mathematics Teacher.*

Using Graphics Software to Create Tessellations

In order to create a tessellation, certain symmetries must be imposed on the figure as it is developed. These symmetries are imposed in two ways. First, every tessellation is developed on a grid that defines the positions of certain points on the final figure. For the tessellations appearing in this example, the grid (Figure 6.29) consists of two vertical bars of equal length, both of which are divided into two equal pieces and joined by a horizontal bar of arbitrary length.

A second set of symmetries is imposed by the rules that govern the types of rotations, reflections, and translations allowed in the creation of the tessellation. Although these transformations may be done using pencil and paper, modern computer graphics make the task much easier. The figures in this example were all done using PC Paint software, an optical mouse, a microcomputer, and a dot matrix printer.

In PC Paint, an edit box may be temporarily drawn around any rectangular portion of the screen. This procedure defines a subset of screen points, all of which may now be modified under a selected transformation. Among the optional transformations, the following are of interest to this discussion: translation of all the points in the edit box to some other location on the screen; reflection of the contents of the edit box along either a vertical or horizontal axis; rotation of the contents of the edit box in ninety-degree increments; replication of the contents of the edit box, with the replica being transferred to any other location on the screen. Using these features, a starting grid like the one shown in Figure 6.29 can be drawn quickly and accurately.

The next step is to define two curves. The first curve is drawn from point *A* to point *B* (Figure 6.30). Like most graphics packages, PC

FIGURE 6.29   Tesselation Starting Grid

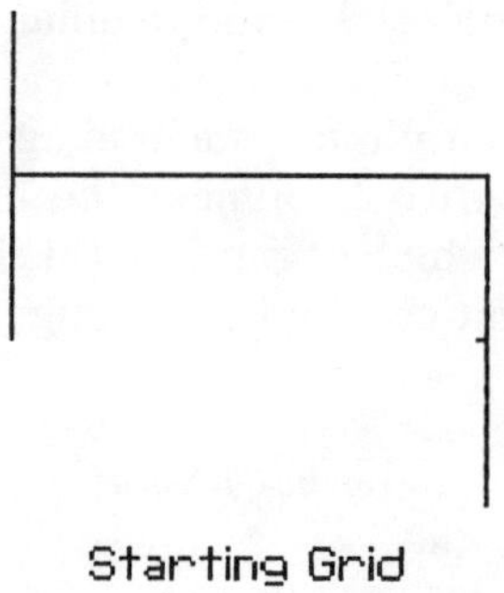

Starting Grid

FIGURE 6.30   **Define Two Curves**

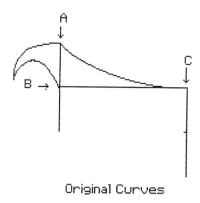

Original Curves

Paint has several options for creating curves and a convenient UNDO command for erasing curves that fail to satisfy. The curve from A to B is accomplished in two steps, using trial and error until a pleasing effect is obtained. Using a similar approach, a second curve is drawn from point A to point C. All further lines in the outline of the tessellation are reflections and translations of these two curves.

The next few steps in the process are illustrated in Figure 6.31. First, the curve from A to B is duplicated below and to the left of the grid by using the COPY feature of the edit box. This curve is then reversed (reflected) from right to left using the FLIP HORIZONTAL command. A similar procedure is used to copy the curve from A to C below the grid and produce its reflection.

The completion of the outline of the tessellation requires that the original curves and their reflections be correctly positioned on the starting grid. This task is accomplished by using PC Paint's COPY feature. The correct placement of these curves is shown in Figure 6.32.

At this point, mathematics has contributed as much as it can to the enterprise. It has produced a tessellating shape that resembles a distorted letter L. To carry the process further, graphics doodlers must invoke their own artistic talents.

Seeing Is More Than Looking

Show Figure 6.32 to several people and ask them what they see. Some individuals see only what is on the paper. Others see more, but that

FIGURE 6.31   Reflect Both Curves

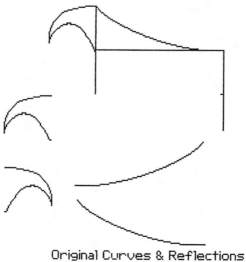

Original Curves & Reflections

"more" comes from within themselves, not from a closer examination of the figure. This ability to recognize similarity of shape between seen and remembered objects leads to identifications like, "a bird" or "an axe head."

Once an association has been formed in the mind of the viewer, the task becomes one of enhancing the figure so everyone can see the

FIGURE 6.32   Position Reflections

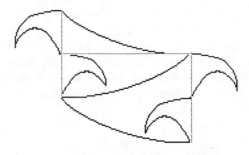

Complete Set of Reflections
And Translations

FIGURE 6.33   Birds of this Feather. . . .

𝕭irds of this 𝕱eather 𝕱lock 𝕿ogether

What symmetries are necessary?

same possibility. This is best done by adding details and shading. In the case of the birds in Figure 6.33, PC Paint's drawing tools were used to shade the beak and body of the bird and to define the eyes and feet.

With some practice, both artistic and mathematical considerations can be considered simultaneously as the tessellation develops. At this point, the graphics doodler has a true multidisciplinary perspective.

FIGURE 6.34   This Could Be a Fish

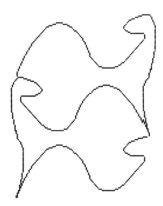

FIGURE 6.35   Tessalasaurus

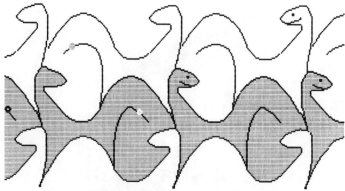

𝕿𝖊𝖘𝖘𝖆𝖑𝖆𝖘𝖆𝖚𝖗𝖚𝖘

An aquatic missing link which begins life
as a fish, then evolves into a dinosaur.
Evolved "schooling" behavior in fish
into "herding" behavior in dinosaurs.

What Does It Look Like?

Figure 6.34 was developed using the procedures outlined in this example. In considering its possibilities, it could be a fish or a dinosaur, so it became both, in Figure 6.35. By varying the shading and details, the objects on the left side of the image begin as fish and gradually change into dinosaurs as the image is scanned from left to right.

Finally, Figure 6.36 is still a work-in-progress. It looks like a seal pup with its mouth open, or it might be a bird in flight, or. . . .

PROBLEM-SOLVING AND CALCULATORS

Although calculating devices play an important role in the world of work and are found in most homes, Table 3.1 shows that relatively few students have access to calculators in school (Dossey, Mullis, Lindquist, and Chambers 1988). This finding is deeply troubling, given the role of calculating devices in modern life and the way that modern technology is changing how mathematics is applied in problem-solving situations. Teachers and parents who choose to ignore these changes and reject the use of calculators and other computing devices in mathemat-

FIGURE 6.36   What Does This Suggest?

ics education are handicapping students in ways that will severely limit the students' future educational and career options.

The position of the National Council of Teachers of Mathematics with regard to the use of modern technology is clearly stated in its *Curriculum and Evaluation Standards for School Mathematics* (1989).

> Because technology is changing mathematics and its uses, we believe that
> - appropriate calculators should be available to all students at all times;
> - a computer should be available in every classroom for demonstration purposes;
> - every student should have access to a computer for individual and group work;
> - students should learn to use the computer as a tool for processing information and performing calculations to investigate and solve problems.

Preparing for Tomorrow

Anyone who has tried to teach children to use calculators knows that, left to themselves, they are uncritical users of the technology. They accept every "answer" without a thought as to its reasonableness. Mental estimates or checking procedures are rarely used. They simply push the buttons and believe the answers, even when the "answers" are absurd. To some teachers and parents, the remedy for this type of uncritical mathematical thinking is to take away the technology and make the students do all their computations on paper. Proponents of this approach also note that this ensures that students continue to practice their basic paper-and-pencil computation skills throughout their school years.

This policy might make sense if the world were not changing. A few decades ago, most people worked in small businesses. Shopkeepers got by with paper-and-pencil arithmetic, and only a few people needed to know anything about higher mathematics and statistics. Today's students will face an entirely different set of tasks when they join the workforce. In the 1990s and beyond, businesses will expect their employees to perform computational tasks requiring advanced mathematical training and sophisticated equipment. Keeping students away from calculators and computers until they start looking for work is not the answer. Training them to use technology effectively *is* the answer. Accomplishing that goal will require the cooperation of every elementary and secondary level mathematics teacher in the country.

SUMMARY

Computer environments like LOGO and the Geometric Supposer series offer students an opportunity to explore geometrical concepts easily. By avoiding time-consuming constructions and measurements, complex figures may be examined quickly for interesting features and relationships. This type of time-saving help is also provided by calculators when students are working on algebraic and numerical problems. In both cases, the student is free to deal with concepts and need not interrupt the search for meaning in order to compute or construct some necessary figure. The opportunity to focus on strategic thinking is one of the most significant benefits of computer technology in mathematics education.

DISCUSSION QUESTIONS

1. How do you feel about teaching students to use calculators and computers? If you are not currently a computer user, what would

it take to convert you? Would you attend inservice training if it was an option? Would you attend a summer workshop? How do your professional colleagues feel about the issue?

2. What does LOGO offer students that drill and practice programs do not offer? How do you feel about open-ended investigations in mathematics? What learning goals do you think are best served by using programs like LOGO and the Geometric Supposer?

3. Tessellations offer mathematics students an opportunity to think spatially rather than numerically and to demonstrate originality of thought. How do you regard this activity? Is it "real"mathematics or something less? Why?

4. Computer graphics are changing the study of geometry in the same way that hand-held calculators changed the study of algebraic mathematics. In both cases, the technology handles computational details, freeing the user to focus on concept development and problem solving. What effect would you like computer graphics to have on the study of mathematics at your grade level(s)? If your students spent more time on concept development and problem solving and less time on paper-and-pencil skills, how would your role as a teacher change?

SUGGESTED READINGS AND REFERENCES

Abelson, Harold, and Andrea diSessa. *Turtle Geometry.* Cambridge, MA: MIT Press, 1981.

Blackhouse, John K. "Fractal Patterns on a Square." *Mathematics in School,* vol. 15, no. 3 (May 1986), 34–37.

Channell, Dwayne E. "Problem Solving with Computers." *The Mathematics Teacher,* vol. 77, No. 7 (Oct. 1984), 534–541.

Curriculum and Evaluation Standards for School Mathematics. Reston, VA: National Council of Teachers of Mathematics, 1989.

Dossey, John A., Ina V. S. Mullis, Mary M. Lindquist, and Donald L. Chambers. *The Mathematics Report Card: Are We Measuring Up?* Princeton, NJ: Educational Testing Service, 1988.

Gill, Steve. "Making Boxes." *The Mathematics Teacher,* vol. 77, no. 7 (Oct. 1984), 526–530.

Kenny, Margaret J., and Stanley J. Bezuszka. *Tessellations Using LOGO.* Palo Alto, CA: Dale Seymour Publications, 1987.

LogoWriter. Logo Computer Systems, Inc. Copyright 1986: New York, NY.

Mandelbrot, Benoit B. *The Fractal Geometry of Nature.* San Francisco: W. H. Freeman, 1982.

Peitgen, H. O., and P. H. Richter. *The Beauty of Fractals.* New York: Springer-Verlag, 1986.

Sawada, Daiyo. "Symmetry and Tessellations from Rotational Transformations on Transparencies." *Arithmetic Teacher,* vol. 33, no. 4, Dec. 1985, 12–13.

Thomas, David A. "Computer Graphics on the Complex Plane: An Introduction to Julia Sets and Fractals." *Computers in Mathematics and Science Teaching,* vol. 7, No. 1–2 (Fall 1987/Winter 1987–88), 29–33.

Thomas, David A. *Math Projects for Young Scientists.* New York: Franklin-Watts. 1988.

Willicut, Bob. "Triangular Tiles for Your Patio?" *Arithmetic Teacher,* vol. 34, no. 9 (May 1987) 43–45.

Zurstadt, Betty K. "Tessellations and the Art of M. C. Escher." *Arithmetic Teacher,* vol. 31, no. 5 (Jan. 1984), 54–55.

CHAPTER 7

Reading, Reasoning, and Problem Solving *

In life, challenging problems rarely present themselves as neatly phrased puzzles. Rather, it is often left to problem-solvers to construct a suitable problem statement as the first step in problem solving.

To a child in school, true problems are generally encountered in the form of word problems, which are, in effect, carefully constructed problem statements. Whether encountered in the study of science or mathematics, these word problems can make extensive interpretive and strategic demands on students. Indeed, it seems reasonable to assume that problem-solving is perceived by some students as being "hard" largely because of the variety of cognitive processes that must be deployed (Nesher 1986).

The role of reading in problem-solving is important enough that

*Used by permission of the *Journal of Reading* (December 1988, pp. 244–249). Published by the International Reading Association.

teachers of science and mathematics should not ignore the linguistic aspects of problem-solving or, for teachers who work in a departmentalized school, pass the problem along to the reading and language arts teachers. On the other hand, science and mathematics teachers do not need to be reading specialists to provide their students with meaningful help in this regard.

DETERMINING HOW WELL JIMMY READS

Many mathematics teachers do not know how to conduct a formal assessment of a student's reading ability or how to obtain an analysis by a third party. Such an assessment is often regarded as a task for reading specialists. On the other hand, soon after the start of school, an observant mathematics teacher may sense which students have a hard time reading. For example, a mathematics teacher might suspect that some students are reading below grade level and that this affects those students' ability to function in mathematics in several ways. Such students may be unable to understand written instructions for exercises in the text and on tests, be unable to follow along in the text when others are reading aloud, and must rely on verbal instruction and direction, making independent work difficult or impossible.

What can a teacher do to identify which students have genuine reading problems? An easy way to identify a student's reading level is to use an Informal Reading Inventory, or IRI, such as Ekwall's (1986). In most cases, IRIs are individually administered and are based upon graded reading passages (passages written at specific grade levels). In a typical passage, a student is asked to read a few paragraphs aloud. During this time, the teacher counts word recognition errors and records the time spent reading. When the student has completed the reading, the teacher asks a series of IRI comprehension questions, comparing the student's answers with answers provided by the IRI. The student's combined score is based on the number of word recognition errors and comprehension question errors. Using this combined score, the teacher can determine whether the student's reading level is the same as, above, or below that of the graded passage.

Of what use is this to mathematics teachers? If the student's general reading skills are well below grade level, the mathematics teacher may have little power to address the student's underlying reading problems. The IRI may be used under such circumstances to establish the need for professional assistance, preferably by a school district reading specialist. Once aware that certain students have such problems, the mathematics teacher should make sure that instructions, tests, and assignments are written in such a way as to make them accessible to all students in the class.

If the student is not reading below grade level, the student's reading problems in mathematics may be related to factors the mathematics teacher has some power to address.

DEALING WITH TECHNICAL VOCABULARY

Word problems make special linguistic demands on the reader, involving both technical terminology and ordinary language. Teachers can focus students' attention on the importance and meaning of technical terminology and thereby formalize and enourage the correct use of technical vocabulary in their thinking.

When presenting a word problem to a class for discussion, ask students for informal, alternative definitions of key words and for interpretations of important phrases. For instance, if a problem asks the reader to find the product of three consecutive, odd integers, the teacher may find general agreement on the meaning of "product" but considerable doubt about exactly what needs to be multiplied. Frequently, this type of group discussion will provide the teacher with valuable information about student misinformation and misconceptions.

Pay particular attention to technical vocabulary and words that may have one meaning in normal discourse and a different meaning in the context of a mathematics problem. For instance, the term "product" is used in common discourse to indicate manufactured goods or the end result of a particular process. This notion is only vaguely related to the use of "product" in mathematics. In some cases, the meaning of technical terms may be illuminated by a consideration of the structure of the word (prefix, root, suffix). The words parallelogram ("parallel" plus "line"), quadrilateral ("four" plus "side"), and octagon ("eight" plus "angle") all contain clues to their meanings.

SEMANTICS: EXTRACTING THE MEANING

In addition to a technical vocabulary, students also need special semantic rules for interpreting mathematical and scientific word problems. Indeed, the complexity of the text itself, rather than the mathematical operations or scientific principles involved, are often the factor that frustrates the problem solver (Kintsch & Greeno 1984; Nesher & Katriel 1977, 1985).

Nesher and Katriel (1977) show that the correct reading of various phrases and terms within word problems depends on an understanding of the logical structure of the text as a whole. Carpenter and Just (1983) reach a similar conclusion, finding that syntactic clues and semantic relations all play a role in determining the meaning of a sentence fragment (word, clause, phrase) and its contribution to the total sentence. Thus, to cope with the complexities of their task, it is not enough for problem-solvers to possess both ordinary linguistic knowledge and a specialized, mathematical and/or scientific vocabulary. They must also employ a specialized semantic knowledge about the way word problem statements are to be read and interpreted.

As an example of the specialized type of language found in mathematics, consider the following problem:

> **Find a three-digit number in which the digits are three consecutive integers such that the product of the digits is eight times the sum of the digits.**

This problem is typical of mathematical statements in that it is concise and precise to those who can interpret it correctly. However, in terms of the familiar forms of normal discourse, the language of this problem is tortured. Most teachers never spend class time teaching students to read and write such passages. As a result, many students do not acquire the specialized, systematic reading skills necessary for interpreting and solving word problems. This may not seem important to students in the seventh grade, but their perspective changes when they reach high school and find out that algebra, chemistry, and physics require students to solve complex mathematical word problems. Too many of these students simply give up on mathematics at this point and thus severely limit their career options.

A simple strategy for focusing class attention on this aspect of problem-solving is to have the students restate the entire problem in their own words. In the case of word problems involving complex grammatical structures, it may help to dissect the original problem into a series of short, simple sentences. For instance, the following interpretive statements might help explain the intent of the sample word problem.

> "You are looking for a three-digit number."
> "The digits are consecutive, like 123 or 789."
> "To test a guess,
>
> 1. Find the sum by adding the digits.
> 2. Multiply the sum of the digits by 8.
> 3. Find the product by multiplying the digits.
> 4. If you get the same result in step 2 and step 3, your three-digit guess is an answer to the problem. If you don't get 8, try another three-digit number."

In developing such statements, students should reflect critically on the substance of the original problem and the accuracy of their own attempt at a restatement. By considering several wordings of the original problem statement, the features and objectives of the problem will be presented in a variety of ways. In this environment, students struggling to grasp the meaning of the problem have the benefit of alternative explanations.

Diagrams, graphs, and other representations are often helpful at this stage. Since students are trying to develop an internal model of the problem, any device, linguistic, pictorial, or graphic, that helps them grasp the conditions and objectives of a problem should be shared with the class as a whole.

For this example, it is helpful to collect data and represent them in tabular form, as in Table 7.1. The possible three-digit numbers appear in the first column, arranged in order so that none are omitted. In the second column, the sum of the digits is computed. The third column shows the product of the digits. The fourth column shows eight times the sum. The purpose of creating such a table is to guarantee that a solution will be found by calculating all possible answers. As shown in the table, only one three-digit number satisfies the conditions of the problem: 456.

Table 7.1   Make a Table

Three-Digit Number	Sum	Product	8*Sum
123	6	6	48
234	9	24	72
345	12	60	96
456	15	120	120
567	18	210	144
678	21	336	168
789	24	504	192

MATHEMATICAL SCHEMATA

Linguistic and semantic knowledge alone are not a sufficient background when it comes to mathematical problem-solving. Mayer (1983) suggests that good problem-solvers also possess an array of mental "templates" which organize incoming information into a familiar framework. In the terminology of cognitive psychology, each such template is called a "schema." Greeno (1980; Greeno and Johnson 1985) discusses schemata in the context of understanding story structures. In this context, a schema provides a type of generic story line that is subsequently filled in with details from the specific story being read. The structure provided by the schema orients the reader to anticipate certain types of information and to place the information in context when it appears. Thus, to comprehend a portion of text, a reader needs to possess an appropriate schema.

As an example, suppose that a reader is handed a short story to read and told it is a mystery. Immediately, the reader anticipates certain features: a crime, a suspect, a sleuth, clues. When starting to read, the reader is alert for these features in the story. However, if the story is really a comedy rather than a mystery, reading will fail to produce the anticipated features. Failure to find what is expected is likely to lead to confusion, then frustration, then a rejection of the "mystery" schema altogether and the adoption of a new schema: comedy. With this new and correct schema, the story can be read and understood.

In Mayer's view (1983), mathematical schemata serve the same function: structuring the way students view and interpret word problems by prompting them to seek certain information and providing a context for the various parts of the problem. Misinterpretation of a word problem may be seen as the consequence of the choice of an inappropriate schema. Studies of expert problem-solvers support Mayer's view. Nesher (1986) discusses experts' use of "control systems" that monitor, and revise as necessary, the experts' choice of schema (identification of problem "type"). With such error control, experts tend to catch their own mistakes very quickly, shifting rapidly to the best available schema for a given problem.

Other researchers (Chi, Feltovich, and Glaser 1980; Resnick 1982, 1984) have shown that novice problem-solvers also process word problems according to their choice of a schema. The difference is that novices have a much smaller set of schemata to choose from and inadequate "control systems" to detect inappropriate choices. Experts may differ from novices primarily in this regard: The experts have a vast library of "templates" and "control systems" that direct and evaluate their choice of schemata, whereas novices have a much smaller selection. In light of these findings, the acquisition of problem-solving schemata and processes to guide the problem-solver in their use seem to be a critical factor in the development of problem-solving skill.

Simon (1980) observes that, by contrast, most algebra texts emphasize procedural knowledge rather than the conditions under which procedures should be applied (schema-type knowledge).

FOSTERING THE CONSTRUCTION OF SCHEMATA

As students go through school, they may come to regard each problem as a unique entity in a universe of unique problems. Teachers can fight this tendency by pointing out the similarities between problems and by encouraging students to look for similarities. For instance, a teacher might say, "Today's problem reminds me of one we looked at last week. Can you guess which problem I'm thinking of?" In the ensuing discussion, both correct and incorrect guesses can be instructive, as the problems are compared. Over time, these discussions could lead to a type of consensus regarding the features of broad classes of problems that tend to occur in mathematics and science. For example, a schema might emerge which recognizes a family of problems in which two moving objects begin their journeys at a common point and travel in opposite directions.

By taking time to consider the similarities and differences between various problems, teachers can encourage students to develop a set of schemata for the interpretation of future problems. Naturally, these templates are of limited use when a student encounters a truly unconventional problem. On the other hand, no merit devolves from glorifying intuition as a substitute for systematic instruction in the recognition and classification of problems.

TEACHING STRATEGY

Teachers should think out loud when analyzing word problems and let students hear them as they categorize a problem (i.e., pick a schema). For instance, the teacher might say, "This reminds me of the motion problem we did yesterday. Both problems involve two vehicles moving away from each other at different velocities. In this problem, the vehicles are cars. Yesterday's problem was about trains. I think the same approach might work for both problems." In this manner, teachers can model the process of associating the features of the problem at hand with a similar problem previously encountered.

Once the teacher has selected a schema appropriate to the problem at hand, let the students listen to a consideration of the different algorithms or operations used in similar situations in the past. For example, "In yesterday's problem, we found out how fast the two trains were separating every hour by adding their speeds. The same approach could be used to find out how fast the cars in this problem are separating. Once we know how fast they are separating, we can calculate how long it will take them to be 120 miles apart."

Teachers should explain their thinking as they test the choice of schema and algorithm. If the first attempt fails, students should be told why it has been rejected and what adjustments are necessary in the approach. Continue this process until the problem has been "solved" and the answer checked.

The point of all this talk is to model two important things: a problem-solving attitude that accepts uncertainty and errors—not as defeats, but as a normal feature of the problem-solving process; and a problem-solving technique that is systematic rather than intuitive.

PRACTICAL PROBLEM-SOLVING STRATEGIES

Teaching problem-solving skills is an important part of an elementary school mathematics teacher's job. Many teachers take a direct approach to this task, teaching students a set of general problem-solving skills, then transfering these skills to a variety of problems. For example, in *Teaching Problem-Solving Strategies* (Dolan and Williamson 1983), the following strategies are presented: guess and check; make a table; patterns; make a model; elimination; and simplify. Each of these strategies constitutes a different approach to problem-solving. By knowing all six strategies, students are more likely to solve problems than if they act on intuition and insight alone.

The "guess and check" strategy requires the student to make a series of calculations. In each calculation, an estimate of some unknown quantity is used to compute the value of a known quantity.

> **Bill has $1.30 in nickels, dimes, and quarters. If he has 9 coins in all, how many of each type of coin does Bill have?**

In solving the problem, the student might guess that Bill has five quarters and the rest in dimes and nickels. A computation is then used to determine that $1.25 is in quarters and the remaining $.05 is in nickels and dimes. At this point, the student should realize that the remaining five cents cannot use up the remaining four coins specified in the problem. Since the original estimate produced an answer that will not satisfy the terms of the problem, the student then modifies the initial guess accordingly, possibly trying three quarters. This quess will lead to a "correct" solution to the problem. (Another solution would be four quarters, one dime, and four nickels.) The important feature of this strategy is that each guess is evaluated then used to generate a better guess, the entire process eventually converging to the correct answer or answers.

The "make a table" strategy was illustrated earlier in this chapter in the three-digit number problem. This approach requires the student to create a table that contains all possible estimates of the variables in a problem. A set of calculations is then completed for each estimate and the results are checked to determine if the conditions of the problem are satisfied. Naturally, this approach will not work when a large number of estimates are possible. In cases where there are only a few possible estimates, this approach works well and is easily done using microcomputer spreadsheet programs that are specifically designed for generating tabular data.

The "patterns" strategy requires students to examine sequences of numbers or geometrical objects in search of some rule that will allow them to extend the sequence indefinitely. For example, students might be asked to find the twentieth term in the sequence that begins

$$1, \quad 1, \quad 2, \quad 3, \quad 5, \quad 8, \quad 13, \ldots .$$

Many problems in mathematics may be solved by using this approach, which is an aspect of inductive thinking—figuring out a rule from examples.

The "make a model" strategy requires the student to construct a physical or conceptual model of some object or process, which is then used to solve the problem.

> **How many different ways can seven squares be arranged in a single shape so that if two squares touch, they share a full side?**

The question may be solved experimentally using cut-out squares as manipulatives. Trying to solve the problem abstractly is both difficult and impractical.

The "elimination" strategy requires the student to use logic to reduce the potential list of answers to a minimum. Using logic, students throw out some potential estimates as unreasonable and focus on the reasonable estimates.

> **Find the number described below:**
> 1. It is divisible by 3.
> 2. It is between 100 and 200.
> 3. It is an odd number.
> 4. The sum of its digits is 6.
> 5. It is divisible by 41.

In this problem, each statement allows the student to rule out many potential answers, leading to the answer 123.

The strategy called "simplify" requires the student to restate the original problem or represent it in some other form (graphical, for example). Once in another form, the problem may submit to one of the other strategies already discussed.

SUMMARY

The first step in solving a mathematical or scientific word problem is to read the problem and interpret the facts, relationships, and goal of the problem correctly. This involves much more than ordinary reading skill. Mathematics and science use specialized vocabularies and state problems in forms rarely encountered in normal discourse or in other subject areas. Furthermore, interpreting a given word problem correctly may require filtering it through a schema that guides the reader in the complex task of sorting facts and relationships in a meaningful and productive manner. Such schemata become bridges between the interpretation of the problem and the selection of an appropriate strategy for solving the problem.

Classroom teachers may occasionally forget that before a solution is possible, the student must first read and interpret the problem correctly. Teachers who perform these tasks without explaining the thought processes involved run the risk of convincing their students that problem-solving is basically intuitive and unteachable. Teachers who demonstrate and explain their reading and thinking behaviors for students to see run the risk of teaching students to think and solve problems systematically and independently. May their tribe increase.

DISCUSSION QUESTIONS

1. How do you analyze a story problem? What routine procedures do you follow to help you interpret the given information and identify what you are looking for? How can you make these procedures "visible" to your students?

2. If you notice that some students are usually unable to solve story problems, even though they are successful on other types of problems, how would you proceed to help these students?

3. Plan a lesson that will teach the strategies "make a table" or "make a model." After you teach the lesson, continue to refer to the strategy for several days whenever appropriate. When the students appear to recognize appropriate occasions for the use of the strategy, plan a lesson to introduce another new strategy.

4. Some students appear to avoid new vocabulary. How can you systematically teach specialized mathematics vocabulary? How can you reward your students for using the vocabulary correctly?

SUGGESTED READINGS AND REFERENCES

Carpenter, P. A., and M. A. Just. "What Your Eyes Do While Your Mind Is Reading." In *Eye Movements in Reading: Perceptual and Language Processes,* edited by Keith Rayner. New York: Academic Press, 1983.

Chi, M. T. H., P. Feltovich, and R. Glaser. "Representation of Physics Knowledge by Experts and Novices." Office of Naval Research Technical Report 2. Pittsburgh: Learning Research and Development Center, University of Pittsburg, 1980.

Dolan, Dan, and James Williamson. *Teaching Problem-Solving Strategies.* Reading, MA: Addison-Wesley, 1983.

Ekwall, Eldon E. *Ekwall Reading Inventory.* 2nd ed. Boston: Allyn and Bacon, 1986.

Greeno, J. G. "Development of Processes for Understanding." Paper presented at the Heidelberg Conference, Heidelberg, Federal Republic of Germany, July 1980.

Greeno, J. G., and W. Johnson. "Competence for Solving and Understanding Problems." ED 263 134. Arlington, VA: ERIC Document Reproduction Service, 1985.

Kintsch, W., and J. G. Greeno. "Understanding and Solving Arithmetic Word Problems." *Psychological Review,* vol. 92, no. 1 (1984), 109–129.

Mayer, R. E. *Thinking, Problem Solving, Cognition.* New York: W. H. Freeman, 1983.

Nesher, P. "Learning Mathematics: A Cognitive Perspective." *American Psychologist,* vol. 41, no. 10 (1986), 1114–1122.

Nesher, P., & T. Katriel. "A Semantic Analysis of Addition and Subtraction Word Problems." *Educational Studies in Mathematics,* vol. 8, no. 3 (1977), 251–269.

Nesher, P., & T. Katriel. "Arithmetic Word Problems: A Textual Approach" (draft). Haifa, Israel: University of Haifa, 1985.

Resnick, L. B. "Syntax and Semantics in Learning to Subtract." In *Addition and Subtraction: A Cognitive Perspective,* edited by T. Carpenter, J. Moser, and T. A. Romberg. Hillsdale, NJ: Lawrence Erlbaum Associates, 1982.

Resnick, L. B. "Beyond Error Analysis: The Role of Understanding in Elementary School Arithmetic." ED 248 099. Arlington, VA: ERIC Document Reproduction Service, 1984.

Simon, Herbert A. "Problem Solving and Education." In *Problem Solving and Education: Issues in Teaching and Learning,* edited by David T. Tuma and Frederick Reif. Hillsdale, NJ: Lawrence Erlbaum Associates, 1980.

CHAPTER 8

Projects and Activities for Home and School

Mathematics activities and projects offer students, teachers, and parents an opportunity to share in the excitement and satisfaction of mathematical exploration. Whether these activities take place during class, after school, or at home, the ideas they generate must find expression. Students need to share what they make, do, or discover with their friends. Teachers should share their experiences with their students and with other teachers. Parents need to take an interest in the mathematical activities of their children and find ways to recognize and reward the children's efforts.

The following activities offer students and teachers a variety of challenging tasks.

ACTIVITY #1

X At school	___ Primary	___ Worksheet(s)
X At home	X Intermediate	___ Manipulatives
X Computers	X Junior high	1 # of periods

NAME OF ACTIVITY   Exploring Fractals

GOAL OR PURPOSE   To familiarize all students with the concept of a fractal and to acquaint older students with the LogoWriter files used to generate fractals.

ASSUMPTIONS   The teacher has read example 2 in chapter 6. The students and teacher have some familiarity with LogoWriter. Older students (and teacher) should have experience writing procedures in LogoWriter.

TEACHER NEEDS   A microcomputer set up for class demonstration. A LogoWriter disk containing the files found in Listings 6.2, 6.4, and 8.1–8.5.

STUDENT NEEDS   All students need unlined paper and pencil. Older students need a photocopy of Listings 6.2, 6.4, and 8.1–8.5. Students who want to try this at home will need a LogoWriter disk like the teacher's.

PROCEDURE(S)   Examine the development of each fractal by using the commands DO 0, DO 1, DO 2, DO 3. Ask the students to draw the generator for each fractal. Older students should examine the listing for each fractal and explain how the generator is produced by using LogoWriter commands.

EXTENSION(S)   What happens to the perimeter of each fractal as it grows? What happens to the area? Try to think of objects in nature that remind you of fractals.

LISTING 8.1   Inverse Snowflake

```
TO START :N
MAKE "X 1
REPEAT :N [ MAKE "X 3*:X ]
MAKE "L 162/:X
CT RG PU HOME HT RT 60 BK 90 LT 30 PD
END


TO DO :N
START :N
REPEAT 3 [ LINE :L RT 120 ]
END


TO LINE :L
IF :N = 0 [FD :L]
IF :N = 1 [MOVE1 :L]
IF :N = 2 [MOVE2 :L]
IF :N = 3 [MOVE3 :L]
IF :N = 4 [MOVE4 :L]
END


TO MOVE1 :L
FD :L RT 60 FD :L LT 120
FD :L RT 60 FD :L
END


TO MOVE2 :L
MOVE1 :L RT 60 MOVE1 :L LT 120
MOVE1 :L RT 60 MOVE1 :L
END


TO MOVE3 :L
MOVE2 :L RT 60 MOVE2 :L LT 120
MOVE2 :L RT 60 MOVE2 :L
END


TO MOVE4 :L
MOVE3 :L RT 60 MOVE3 :L LT 120
MOVE3 :L RT 60 MOVE3 :L
END
```

LISTING 8.2   Cross Fractal

```
TO START :N
MAKE "X 1
REPEAT :N [ MAKE "X 3*:X ]
MAKE "L 160/:X
CT RG PU HT BK 30 RT 60 BK 90 LT 60 PD
END

TO DO :N
START :N
REPEAT 4 [ LINE :L RT 90 ]
END

TO LINE :L
IF :N = 0 [FD :L]
IF :N = 1 [MOVE1 :L]
IF :N = 2 [MOVE2 :L]
IF :N = 3 [MOVE3 :L]
IF :N = 4 [MOVE4 :L]
END

TO MOVE1 :L
FD :L RT 90 FD :L LT 90
FD :L LT 90 FD :L RT 90
FD :L
END

TO MOVE2 :L
MOVE1 :L RT 90 MOVE1 :L LT 90
MOVE1 :L LT 90 MOVE1 :L RT 90
MOVE1 :L
END

TO MOVE3 :L
MOVE2 :L RT 90 MOVE2 :L LT 90
MOVE2 :L LT 90 MOVE2 :L RT 90
MOVE2 :L
END

TO MOVE4 :L
MOVE3 :L RT 90 MOVE3 :L LT 90
MOVE3 :L LT 90 MOVE3 :L RT 90
MOVE3 :L
END
```

LISTING 8.3   Flower Fractal

```
TO DO :N
START :N
REPEAT 3 [LINE :L RT 120]
END

TO START :N
MAKE "X 1
REPEAT :N [ MAKE "X 3*:X ]
MAKE "L 108/:X
CT RG PU HOME HT RT 60 BK 50 LT 30 PD
END

TO LINE :L
IF :N = 0 [FD :L]
IF :N = 1 [MOVE1 :L]
IF :N = 2 [MOVE2 :L]
IF :N = 3 [MOVE3 :L]
IF :N = 4 [MOVE4 :L]
END

TO MOVE1 :L
LT 45 FD :L*1.414 RT 45 FD :L
RT 45 FD :L*1.414 LT 45
END

TO MOVE2 :L
LT 45 MOVE1 :L*1.414 RT 45 MOVE1 :L
RT 45 MOVE1 :L*1.414 LT 45
END

TO MOVE3 :L
LT 45 MOVE2 :L*1.414 RT 45 MOVE2 :L
RT 45 MOVE2 :L*1.414 LT 45
END

TO MOVE4 :L
LT 45 MOVE3 :L*1.414 RT 45 MOVE3 :L
RT 45 MOVE3 :L*1.414 LT 45
END
```

LISTING 8.4   Island Fractal

```
TO DO :N
START :N
REPEAT 3 [LINE :L RT 120]
END

TO START :N
MAKE "X 1
REPEAT :N [ MAKE "X 3*:X ]
MAKE "L 81/:X
CT RG PU HOME HT RT 60 BK 50 LT 30 PD
END

TO LINE :L
IF :N = 0 [FD :L]
IF :N = 1 [MOVE1 :L]
IF :N = 2 [MOVE2 :L]
IF :N = 3 [MOVE3 :L]
IF :N = 4 [MOVE4 :L]
END

TO MOVE1 :L
FD :L
LT 60
FD 2*:L
RT 120
FD 2*:L
LT 60
END

TO MOVE2 :L
MOVE1 :L
LT 60
MOVE1 :L
MOVE1 :L
RT 120
MOVE1 :L
MOVE1 :L
LT 60
END
```

LISTING 8.4   Cont'd

```
TO MOVE3 :L
MOVE2 :L
LT 60
MOVE2 :L
MOVE2 :L
RT 120
MOVE2 :L
MOVE2 :L
LT 60
END

TO MOVE4 :L
MOVE3 :L
LT 60
MOVE3 :L
MOVE3 :L
RT 120
MOVE3 :L
MOVE3 :L
LT 60
END
```

ACTIVITY #2

X At school	___ Primary	___ Worksheet(s)
X At home	___ Intermediate	___ Manipulatives
X Computers	X Junior high	3 # of periods

NAME OF ACTIVITY   Modifying Fractals

GOAL OR PURPOSE   Using a few geometrical concepts and a little insight, students may create a new fractal by making simple changes in the listing of an existing fractal.

LISTING 8.5   Dragon Curve Fractal

```
TO DO :N
START :N
REPEAT 4 [LINE :L RT 90]
END


TO START :N
MAKE "X 1
REPEAT :N [MAKE "X 4*:X ]
MAKE "L 112/:X
CT RG PU HT BK 12 RT 60 BK 90 LT 60 PD
END


TO LINE :L
IF :N = 0 [FD :L]
IF :N = 1 [MOVE1 :L]
IF :N = 2 [MOVE2 :L]
IF :N = 3 [MOVE3 :L]
END


TO MOVE1 :L
FD :L LT 90 FD :L RT 90
FD :L RT 90 FD 2*:L LT 90
FD :L LT 90 FD :L RT 90
FD :L
END


TO MOVE2 :L
MOVE1 :L LT 90 MOVE1 :L RT 90
MOVE1 :L RT 90 MOVE1 :L MOVE1 :L LT 90
MOVE1 :L LT 90 MOVE1 :L RT 90
MOVE1 :L
END


TO MOVE3 :L
MOVE2 :L LT 90 MOVE2 :L RT 90
MOVE2 :L RT 90 MOVE2 :L MOVE2 :L LT 90
MOVE2 :L LT 90 MOVE2 :L RT 90
MOVE2 :L
END
```

ASSUMPTIONS Students and teacher have experience writing LogoWriter procedures and have completed the activity exploring fractals (example 2 in chapter 6).

TEACHER NEEDS A microcomputer set up for class demonstration. A LogoWriter disk containing the files found in Listings 6.2, 6.4, and 8.1–8.5.

STUDENT NEEDS All students need a photocopy of Listings 6.2, 6.4, and 8.1–8.5. Students who want to try this at home will need a LogoWriter disk like the teacher's.

PROCEDURE(S) Follow the suggestions for home-grown fractals found in example 2 in chapter 6. This involves changing the shape of the original polygon from, say, a triangle to a square. Students may also experiment with changing the size of the image. More capable students may wish to experiment with the shape of the generator, defined for each fractal in the procedure MOVE1 and echoed in the other MOVE procedures. A comparison of Listing 6.2 and Listing 8.1 will reveal the manner in which the two generators are related; one uses a triangular "bump out," and the other uses the same shape as a "bump in."

EXTENSION(S) As students create new fractals, have them print out the objects and the LogoWriter procedures that made them. Post these on a bulletin board. Have a contest for the most interesting fractals, most beautiful, strangest, and so forth.

ACTIVITY #3

X At school	X Primary	X Worksheet(s)
X At home	X Intermediate	X Manipulatives
___ Computers	X Junior high	2 # of periods

NAME OF ACTIVITY Beginning Boxes

GOAL OR PURPOSE To introduce students to the concept of the volume of a rectangular solid.

ASSUMPTIONS Familiarity with the centimeter as a unit of measurement.

TEACHER NEEDS Several sheets of centimeter graph paper, ruler, scissors, pencil, tape, sugar cubes 1 cm on a side.

STUDENT NEEDS Several sheets of centimeter graph paper, ruler, scissors, pencil, tape, sugar cubes 1 cm on a side.

PROCEDURE(S) Following the procedures outlined in "A Concrete Approach" in Example 1 of Chapter 6, demonstrate for the class the construction of a rectangular solid. Fill the solid with sugar cubes and express the volume both as a number (of cubes) and as a bar graph (of cubes). Following the demonstration, create teams of three or four students and assign each team the task of making all the possible solids for a given starting grid by using integer corner cuts. Have each team record their findings in a table and bar graph. When all the data have been collected, look for a pattern. Most classes should realize that the volume can be calculated using the formula

Volume = Length * Width * Height

EXTENSION(S) Ask if there seems to be a largest possible volume for each starting grid. Ask about fractional corner cuts. Would the solid still have volume? If so, what kind of numerical answer would you expect to get?

ACTIVITY #4

X	At school	___	Primary	___	Worksheet(s)
X	At home	X	Intermediate	___	Manipulatives
X	Computers	X	Junior high	2	# of periods

NAME OF ACTIVITY **Computer Boxes**

GOAL OR PURPOSE   To extend the concept of volume developed in the Beginning Boxes activity to include solids with sides that are not integers.

ASSUMPTIONS   Students and teacher have done the Beginning Boxes activity.

TEACHER NEEDS   A microcomputer suitable for class demonstration and a LogoWriter disk containing the procedures found in Listing 6.1.

STUDENT NEEDS   Access to a computer and the same disk used by the teacher.

PROCEDURE(S)   Demonstrate the computer simulation explained in example 1 of chapter 6, using as examples starting grids and corner cuts already investigated by the students in the beginning boxes activity. Once the students understand what the program does, move the discussion to the subject of decimal corner cuts. Demonstrate this feature by using the computer simulation and discuss the meaning of the bar graph. Assign groups of students the task of investigating decimal corner cuts for specific starting grids, with the goal of finding the largest possible box. Have the students print out their final graph and write down the volumes listed at the bottom of the screen. These data should be presented as a table to accompany the graph. These materials should then be posted on a bulletin board and shared in class discussion.

EXTENSION(S)   Discuss the investigation in the context of a manufacturer who wants to build a box for shipping foam packaging material ("popcorn"). Does the shape of the box have anything to do with the cost of materials for manufacturing the box?

ACTIVITY #5

X	At school	X	Primary	X	Worksheet(s)
X	At home	X	Intermediate	X	Manipulatives
	Computers	X	Junior high	1	# of periods

NAME OF ACTIVITY   Introduction to the Geoboard

GOAL OR PURPOSE   To orient students in the use of the geoboard and dot paper and to investigate the area of rectangular objects.

ASSUMPTIONS   Students are ready to consider the concept of area.

TEACHER NEEDS   Geoboard and rubber bands. A transparent geoboard on an overhead projector is helpful when it comes to demonstrations. A worksheet consisting of objects like those shown in Figure 8.1, which may be covered by using only rectangular objects.

STUDENT NEEDS   Geoboard and rubber bands. Dot paper (See Figure 8.2)

PROCEDURE(S)

1. Free investigation. Five minutes to create designs on the geoboard.
2. Shape duplication. Students should be asked to duplicate a variety of convex and concave polygons. Start with easy shapes and finish with complex figures. This requires students to fo-

FIGURE 8.1   **Break into Rectangular Areas**

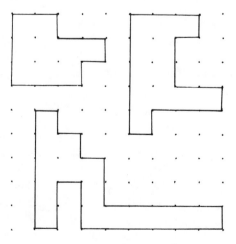

FIGURE 8.2   Dot Paper

cus on specific attributes of the polygons. Record results on dot paper. 15 minutes.

3. Make a square which is one unit on a side and discuss its area. Use this unit of area to "count" the area of several simple rectangular objects.

4. Rectangular areas. Give students a worksheet (see Figure 8.1) on dot paper, showing several shapes that can be divided into squares and rectangles. Ask students to find the area of each shape. 15 minutes.

EXTENSION(S) Have students create complex shapes that may be divided into squares and rectangles. Find the area of each shape. Record shapes and areas on dot paper.

ACTIVITY #6

X	At school		Primary	X	Worksheet(s)
X	At home	X	Intermediate	X	Manipulatives
	Computers	X	Junior high	1	# of periods

NAME OF ACTIVITY   Triangular Areas

GOAL OR PURPOSE   To introduce the concept of the area of a right triangular object.

ASSUMPTIONS   Students have completed the introduction to the geoboard activity.

TEACHER NEEDS   Geoboard and rubber bands.

STUDENT NEEDS   Geoboard and rubber bands. Dot paper (See Figure 8.2)

PROCEDURE(S)

1. Have the students make a square that is one unit on a side. Review the manner in which this square unit was used to determine the area of rectangular objects in the Introduction to the Geoboard activity.

2. Divide the unit square in half along a diagonal and discuss the area of the triangular pieces. Note that the triangles are right triangles. Next, make a 1-by-2 rectangle and divide it in half along a diagonal. Discuss the area of the right triangular pieces. Repeat with a variety of rectangles. Have each student create a right triangle in this manner and determine its area.

3. Ask the class to create two different right triangles, each with area 2 square units. The most likely answers involve the following rectangles: 1-by-4; 2-by-2.

4. Ask the class to create interesting objects that may be subdivided into rectangular and right-triangular areas. The area of each object should then be determined. Record the objects and their areas on dot paper.

EXTENSION(S)   Create a 3-by-4 rectangle. Next, loop a rubber band over one 4 unit side and the middle nail on the opposite side. Note that this forms three triangles. Two of these are right triangles. Is the third triangle a right triangle? How would the area of the third triangle be determined?

ACTIVITY #7

X At school	___ Primary	X Worksheet(s)
X At home	X Intermediate	X Manipulatives
___ Computers	X Junior high	1 # of periods

NAME OF ACTIVITY More Triangles

GOAL OR PURPOSE To investigate the areas of triangles other than right triangles.

ASSUMPTIONS Students have done the Triangular Areas activity.

TEACHER NEEDS Geoboard and rubber bands, a worksheet consisting of objects like those shown in Figure 8.3.

STUDENT NEEDS Geoboard, rubber bands, and dot paper.

FIGURE 8.3   Break into Triangular Areas

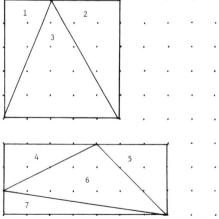

PROCEDURE(S)

1. Determine the area of right triangles 1 and 2 in Figure 8.3.

2. Discuss whether triangle 3 is a right triangle. Because it is not, discuss the need for a new strategy. Two ideas commonly arise: divide triangle 3 into two right triangles; or find the area of the rectangle containing triangles 1, 2, and 3, then subtract the areas of triangle 1 and 2 from the area of the rectangle. Both strategies should be discussed and tested.

3. Discuss a strategy for finding the area of triangle 6.

4. Ask students to make up and solve problems like these and present their findings to the class.

EXTENSION(S) Modify the figure containing triangles 1 - 3 so that the "peak" of triangle 3 is shifted one nail to the left. Determine the area of the new triangle 3. Discuss your findings. Make another triangle that has the same area as triangle 3.

ACTIVITY #8

X At school	___ Primary	X Worksheet(s)
X At home	___ Intermediate	X Manipulatives
___ Computers	X Junior high	1 # of periods

NAME OF ACTIVITY Give Me a Square

GOAL OR PURPOSE To create a square of a given area.

ASSUMPTIONS Students are familiar with the Pythagorean Theorem.

TEACHER NEEDS Geoboard and rubber bands.

STUDENT NEEDS Geoboard, rubber bands, and dot paper.

PROCEDURE(S)

1. Show a square with area 1 and square with area 4. Ask for squares with area 9, 16, and 25. Make a point of identifying the length of the sides of these squares.

2. Ask for a square with area 2. What length side will it have? Using the Pythagorean Theorem, point out that the diagonal distance between the nails on the geoboard is the square root of 2.

3. Ask for a square with area 5. With area 8. With area 10. Record findings on dot paper.

4. Ask students to discover other squares and record the objects and their areas on dot paper.

EXTENSION(S) What is the largest square that can be constructed on your geoboard other than the square around all the nails?

ACTIVITY #9

X	At school	___	Primary	___	Worksheet(s)
X	At home	X	Intermediate	X	Manipulatives
___	Computers	X	Junior high	1	# of periods

NAME OF ACTIVITY   Tessellating the Plane

GOAL OR PURPOSE   To demonstrate that any convex quadrilateral will tessellate the plane.

ASSUMPTIONS   Students are familiar with the concept of a 180 degree rotation about a point.

TEACHER NEEDS   Figures 8.4 and 8.5 on acetate and an overhead projector; four additional construction paper cutous of Figure 8.4.

FIGURE 8.4   Random Convex Quadrilateral

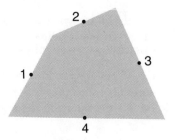

STUDENT NEEDS   Construction paper and scissors.

PROCEDURE(S)

1. Using Figure 8.4 as an example on the overhead projector, discuss the meaning of "convex quadrilateral." Note that points 1–4 mark the midpoints of the sides of the convex quadrilateral.

FIGURE 8.5   Tessellating the Plane

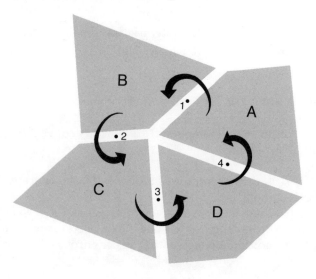

2. Place Figure 8.5 on the overhead projector. Point out that objects *A*, *B*, *C*, and *D* are identical except for their positions on the page. Lay Figure 8.4 on top of Figure 8.5 and show how a 180° rotation of object *A* about point 1 produces object *B*. Then rotate object *B* about point 2 to obtain object *C*. Finally, rotate object *C* about point 3 to obtain object *D*.

3. It is now clear that the objects will fit together at one point in the plane. Using your additional cutouts, complete the effect at every vertex of the original object.

4. It should now be clear that the original convex quadrilateral will tile the plane. What about the new object formed by joining four of the original objects? Will it tessellate the plane? Are any rotations necessary?

5. Have each student create a different convex quadrilateral, making several copies. Each student should then arrange the objects to tessellate the plane and tape the object to a piece of paper. These should then be displayed for all to see and enjoy.

EXTENSION(S) Why does every convex quadrilateral tessellate the plane? Measure the angles of each quadrilateral. What do you always get? Does that guarantee that the figures will fit together perfectly at a point?

ACTIVITY #10

X	At school	X	Primary		Worksheet(s)
X	At home	X	Intermediate	X	Manipulatives
	Computers		Junior high	1	# of periods

NAME OF ACTIVITY Attribute Guess

GOAL OR PURPOSE Guess the sorting rule being used by another student.

ASSUMPTIONS Students are familiar with attribute materials.

TEACHER NEEDS   Attribute materials.

STUDENT NEEDS   Attribute materials.

PROCEDURE(S)

1. Begin placing one object at a time on the table. The objects should be arranged in a line. As the sorter, you select each object so that it differs from the last one in line on exactly one attribute—say, color. This means that successive objects will have the same shape and size. The point is for students to guess your sorting rule. Keep placing objects in line until a student guesses your sorting rule.

2. The student who correctly guesses your rule then assumes the role of sorter, using a different rule. Continue the demonstration until a student guesses the second sorting rule.

3. Now divide the class into groups of four to six students. One student in each group takes turns acting as sorter while the rest try to guess the rule. It often helps to have a referee at each table; this student is told the sorting rule before the start of each object train. If the referee thinks the sorter has made a mistake, he or she checks with the sorter to make sure the sorting rule is being used consistently. When a student guesses the rule, the referee may confer with the sorter to determine if the guess is correct.

EXTENSION(S)   After beginning with simple sorting rules, try more complex rules.

Glossary of Terms and Expressions

Absorption theory of learning   In this theory, knowledge equals facts identified by an authority, and learning is a kind of mental copying process in which the learner attempts to memorize the facts supplied by the authority. Extensive use is made of stimulus-response methodologies.

Abstract random   One of four learning styles in Gregorc's model; characterized by sensitivity to emotional, social, and artistic concerns and by a dislike of regimentation.

Abstract sequential   One of four learning styles in Gregorc's model; characterized by an orientation to analytical thinking and the organization of ideas.

Analytic skill   The ability to interpret the various parts of a complex problem statement correctly.

Attribute materials   A collection of objects or shapes sharing various geometrical or other properties or attributes; used in sorting activities.

Circumference   The distance around a circle.

Cognitive theory of learning   In this theory, knowledge equals internal representations created by the learner and acquired through active analysis of data, sensory impressions, and so forth. Extensive use is made of dialogue, manipulative materials, and so on.

Commutative   If an operation is commutative, reversing the order of the terms does not change the answer (for example, $4 \times 5 = 5 \times 4$; $2 + 3 = 3 + 2$).

Computer model   A computer program that simulates some complex mathematical procedure.

Concrete operations   A Piagetian stage of intellectual development characteristic of elementary school children. Normally begins about age seven.

Concrete random   One of four learning styles in Gregorc's model; characterized by a creative orientation to hands-on, practical tasks.

Concrete sequential   One of four learning styles in Gregorc's model; characterized by a preference for a routine, systematic, detail-oriented approach to life.

Decimal numeration   A topic dealing with the meaning assigned to the various place values in whole numbers and decimals.

Deductive thinking   Reasoning from rules to specific cases; also called "top-down" thinking.

Diagonal   A line connecting two nonconsecutive corners of a polygon.

Difference   The answer to a subtraction problem.

Egocentric   Focused on oneself.

Exterior angle   The angle formed outside a polygon when a side of the polygon is extended beyond a vertex.

Formal operations   A Piagetian stage of intellectual development, characterized by abstract thought. Normally begins about age eleven or twelve.

Fractal   A mathematical object, usually a figure, that is self-similar.

Generator segment   Used to define the nature of the self-similarity of a fractal.

Geoboard   A sheet of wood or plastic with a square array of nails or pegs perpendicular to the surface. Rubber bands are stretched between the nails to define geometrical shapes.

Hexagon   A six-sided polygon.

Hypotenuse   The longest side on a right triangle; opposite the right angle.

Inductive thinking   Reasoning from specific examples to generalizations; also known as "bottom-up" thinking.

Information-processing approach   A research methodology that seeks to identify in detail all the thoughts and behaviors students employ while performing a task.

Initiator segment   Used to define the object from which a self-similar object is developed.

Interior angle   An angle inside a polygon formed by two consecutive sides.

Irrational number   Any number, such as pi, that cannot be expressed as the ratio of two integers.

Learning style   A habitual approach to thinking and learning.

Line of symmetry   A line through an object that divides the object so that both halves of the object are identical and oriented in the same direction with respect to the line of symmetry. For example, the capital letters, A,W,T,Y,U,O,H,X,V,M all have a vertical line of symmetry that divides them in half so that each half is a mirror image of the other half.

LOGO   A computer language developed for the investigation of geometrical objects by children.

Manipulative object   Any object used by children to model some process or to clarify their thinking about some concept.

Math anxiety   A disabling fear of one's inadequate ability to do mathematics.

Metacognition   Thinking about one's own thinking; critical analysis of the strength of one's own arguments.

Number line   A straight line with the integers located at evenly spaced intervals.

Numeration materials   A set of manipulative objects used to model the meaning of the units, tens, and hundreds places in discussions of arithmetic operations.

N-gon   A polygon having N sides, where N is any whole number.

Octagon   A polygon having eight sides.

Parallel   Two lines in the same plane that never intersect.

Part-whole thinking   Thinking that recognizes the relationships between different sets of objects and their subsets.

Pattern blocks   A set of polygons used as manipulative materials in the study of shapes.

Perimeter   The distance around an object.

Plane   A flat, two-dimensional surface extending indefinitely without edge or crease.

Polygon   Triangle, square, hexagon, and so forth; a shape having any number of sides.

Preoperational   The Piagetian stage of intellectual development common among preschool children, roughly ages two to six.

Prime   A whole number that is not evenly divisible by any whole number other than one and itself.

Product   The answer to a multiplication problem.

Pythagorean Theorem   If a right triangle has sides of length a and b and hypotenuse of length c, then $a^2 + b^2 = c^2$.

Rational number   A number that can be represented as the ratio of two integers.

Reflection   A geometrical transformation that flips an object about a reflection line, reversing the orientation of the object, just as a mirror reverses a person's features from right to left.

Regrouping Carrying and borrowing in arithmetic.

Right angle A 90° angle, formed by two perpendicular lines.

Rotation A geometrical transformation that turns an object about some point.

Schemata Collections of knowledge structures (problem types, story lines, procedures) used to classify new information according to known patterns.

Self-similarity A property in which small parts of some object resemble larger parts of the same object; a repetition of some theme on several scales or magnifications.

Semantics The study of the meaning of words and statements.

Sensorimotor A Piagetian stage of intellectual development that extends from birth to about age two.

Simulation An imitation of some process; often a computer program that imitates some mathematical process.

Stimulus-response approach An approach to training that seeks to strengthen the learner's associations between questions and answers by repeated drill and practice.

Story problem A word problem.

Sum The answer to an addition problem.

Tessellation A single interlocking figure that will cover the plane.

Tiling Any combination of figures that will cover the plane.

Translation A geometrical transformation that slides an object from one location in the plane to another without any rotation or reflection.

Vertex A corner of a polygon, where two sides intersect.

Whole number 0, 1, 2, 3, 4, 5, and so on.

Word problem A mathematical problem presented in the form of written or spoken language and requiring significant interpretive skill.

Index